journal

belongs to:

_____

Thank you for purchasing
MY GYMNASTICS JOURNAL
52 weeks of goals, growth, and gratitude.

It is my genuine hope that this journal can help you grow as a person and a gymnast.

Love what you do! Do what you love!

Please share your story with me
through email or social media.
Email me at srfabricoauthor@gmail.com,
and I will send you a free inspirational coloring page.

For bulk discount orders, email srfabricoauthor@gmail.com

Let's get social!

- @srfabricoauthor
- @myjournalseries
- @srfabrico_author
- @the_myjournalseries
- @srfabrico_author
- S.R. Fabrico
- srfabricoauthor@gmail.com
- srfabrico.com

PRAISE FOR MY GYMNASTICS JOURNAL

"My Journal Series is the best resource for young athletes in all sports to set goals and chart their own progress. Documenting these goals, highs and lows, progress, and achievements teaches them a lot about life and planning for their own success."
~ Steve Butcher, Olympic Coach, and Judge

"Weekly goal setting is an important part of Flip Fest Gymnastics Camp. As former Olympians, we believe setting goals is an important part of achieving success. My Gymnastics Journal helps athletes do just that."
~ John Macready & John Roethlisberger, Owner Flip Fest Camps, and Former Olympians

"The My Journal Series is a MUST! So many good books have been written concerning youth sports, but this is one I highly recommend. It should be at the top of everyone's list, whether you're a coach, parent, mentor, friend, athlete, or non-athlete. I've coached athletes for over forty years, ranging from beginner to Olympian. My Gymnastics Journal is a book that is truly engaging, teaches valuable life skills, and is certainly one that everyone will enjoy."
~ Phil Savage, Six time Hall of Fame gymnastics coach and fourteen years USA Men's Junior National Team coach

"Regardless of whether you're setting goals for your sport or for your life, I found My Journal Series will be extremely helpful in getting you there!"
~ Lisa Savage, Business owner and Gymnastic coach for over 40 years and Hall of Fame Inductee

"My Gymnastics Journal is a fantastic book for gymnasts who want to succeed in their sport. This journal gives gymnasts a guided tool to set and achieve goals throughout their season. In addition, teaches them about gratitude and reflection which in turn helps build self-esteem. The joy is in the journey and My Gymnastics Journal helps the athlete remember that."
~ Mike Martinez, Owner - Ozone Leotards

"My Journal Series is like having a Sensei walking side by side with you softly guiding you to the water of your own mind. What a creative way to build a gracious attitude and expand your perspective of yourself as a dancer.

If only I had known the importance of a positive mindset when I first started as a dancer. My Dance Journal is a streamlined way to develop good habits early on in your dance journey or career."
~ Bettis Richardson, Choreographer, Dancer, and Entertainer

"Journaling - a daily walk through our journey! One of the best stress reduction tools for athletes is to write in your journal each day. By setting incremental goals, we stay motivated to keep striving for that ultimate goal! Writing down short-range and long-range goals, with plans on how to achieve them, keeps us on task. Writing five things you are grateful for each

day is also a stress reliever. Journaling keeps our cognitive brain working so our emotions cannot hijack our thought processes."
~ Debbie Love, International Clinician in Injury Prevention Conditioning, Sports Psychology, Flexibility and Technical Tumbling

"As a coach for over twenty years, I have always found it important for my athletes to journal for numerous reasons. One of those reasons is accountability. Being accountable to yourself is not only a feeling of pride, but also a feeling of honesty. Journaling is a simple habit that will allow you to become self-aware and identify patterns in your skills and your practice. The My Cheer Journal will help you focus on being positive, set attainable goals, and be gracious!"
~ Sean Timmons, Nfinity Athletic, Cheerleading Brand Director

"I am excited for the publishing of My Cheer Journal. I think this will be a great tool for athletes, coaches, and parents to motivate and measure goals and progress for cheer training. I am excited to introduce this to The Stingray Allstars!"
~ Casey Jones, President – Stingray Cheer Company

"The My Journal Series is tremendous for all sports. This isn't just any journal, My Journal Series guides athletes through the steps making it easy for them to follow! The author did a brilliant job putting this together for a variety of ages and sports. I highly recommend teams or individuals to check out My Journal Series."
~ Cole Stott, Owner - Premier Athletics

"My Dance Journal is brilliant and is great for all ages! It's a perfect tool for dancers to track their goals, have self-reflection, and measure growth. It's also an awesome opportunity for coaches to connect with their dancers and see what their little minds are thinking! Parents can also help track their dancers' progress by following along as well. We are so excited to be using these with all of our dancers this season!"
~ Dana Parson, Owner - Dance Mania All-Stars

"Wow! My Journal Series is an awesome opportunity for athletes to set themselves up for a successful season and look back on their journey. I wish that I'd had one of these when I was a dancer. I love that the My Journal Series has a variety of options geared to specific sports. I encourage athletes to check out the My Journal Series."
~ Anastasia Miller Burns, Executive Vice President – Inside Magazine

"Parents: Do you want to help your dancer grow and develop not only into a better technician but also a leader?

Coaches: Have you been looking for a team building activity to not only motivate your dancers but also encourage them to be better teammates and leaders?

This timely journal/goal setting/character building book is a must for students who are leaving a time of solitary Zoom environments and reentering daily practices and working with other teenagers.

The tools provided allow not only for introspection but also encourage reaching out to assist other team members, saying thank you to teachers, coaches, and those who assist them along their journey, and being intentional in taking care of their bodies through hydration.

Excited to see where this book leads our upcoming generation of dancers who become coaches and teachers, I believe it is a powerful tool to enhance the character-building traits of our art."

~ Mary Wendt, Texas Dance Educators and National Dance Coaches Association Hall of Fame recipient, National and International adjudicator, leadership curriculum facilitator and developer, and dance industry professional for over forty years

"Success at anything takes a well calculated plan. With My Dance Journal, S.R. Fabrico has provided a roadmap that focuses on your journey to success. By using this tool, any athlete from any sport can capitalize on what it takes to be GREAT at your craft. Coaching cheerleaders and dancers for over forty years, I can tell you from experience that the winners do what it takes to improve daily. You cannot improve if you do not know what needs improving and have a roadmap to reflect on your journey, turn your weaknesses into strengths, and set goals to obtain the greatness you desire. Successful athletes work as hard on the mental aspects of their crafts as they do the physical. Take advantage of this easy to use, helpful, fun tool to not only develop your physical skills but also your mental aptitude as well. Happy journaling!"

~ Glenda Broderick, Southeast Regional Director, United States All-Star Federation

"As a professional dancer and teacher within this industry for over seventeen years, journaling, meditation, and visualization have been a quintessential part of my personal growth and development. My Dance Journal helps to create a mental awareness to increase the likelihood of students achieving their goals through introspection and reflection. By asking the right questions and identifying their own challenges, this book creates a proactive resolve to help students achieve their own goals within dance. It's safe to say that growth is an uncomfortable process, and pain is a necessary investment for progress. Having a guided journal can give students the tools they need to accomplish their goals. Please give your children the gift that will help them develop mature performance qualities that will bring out the best in themselves and others!"
  ~ N'tegrity Quinones, N'tegrity in Motion Entertainment and Dance Education

"The My Dance Journal provides the perfect tools and guidance to assist any dancer along the path to achieve goals. By goal setting, tracking, and reflecting on accomplishments and setbacks, one will see growth not only as a dancer, but also as an individual!"
~ Janna Thomas, The Dance Connection

"This one-of-a-kind dance journal will be a hit for any age dancer. What this book can teach a dancer on and off the stage will last a lifetime. It not only educates dancers about their sport but also encourages self-motivation, goal setting, and much more. My Dance Journal is here to push your favorite dancer to grow and learn in mind, body, and spirit!"
~ Cheryl Passalacqua, Stage 8 Dance Brands

"Journaling began as a way to keepsake memories for me, but now it's transformed into so much more! It's a way to express my feelings and work through struggles or to help create a better me! I look forward to reading My Firefly Journal and all of the amazing advice it will bring into my life. My Journal Serieswill be great for athletes, especially this day in age when so many people are struggling to find a way to have their voice be heard!"
~ Erin Nicely, Sports Mom

"Swimming is a journey, not a destination. Make sure you set a firm foundation, you trust in the processes of your coach and yourself, and you remain ready to grow through your failures and successes. If you set the right building blocks, your dreams and goals can come true. My Swim Journal is a fantastic tool to help with all of the above."
~ James Gallagher, FAST Head Age Group Coach and General Chair Southern California Swimming

"My daughter's coach required his team to journal about their practices. My daughter really had no idea how to get her thoughts out and make it easy to reflect back on previous practices. But then I found My Swim Journal, and it became a complete game changer! Everything about the journal made it fun for her to add her entries and continue to journal throughout the season! The bonus was there was a place to reflect on meets and keep track of personal times. This journal is amazing, and I highly recommend it to all swimmers and coaches!"
~ Steph Della Costa, Swim Mom

MY GYNASTICS JOURNAL

52 weeks of goals, growth, and gratitude

S.R. Fabrico

Copyright © 2022 S. R. Fabrico All rights reserved.

This book contains material protected under international and federal copyright laws and treaties. Any unauthorized report or use of this material is prohibited. No part of this book may be reproduced or transmitted in any form or by any means, electronic or mechanical, including photocopying, recording, or by any information storage and retrieval system without express written permission from the author/publisher.

Mentions of public figures in this book do not imply endorsement by the author or publisher. The information in this book should not be treated as a substitute for medical advice. Neither the author nor publisher can be held responsible for any loss, claim, or damage from the use, misuse, or suggestions made in the contents within this book. In event you use any information in this book for yourself, the author and the publisher assume no responsibility for your actions.

PAPERBACK ISBN: 979-8-9864787-4-6
HARDBACK ISBN: 979-8-9864787-5-3

Published by: SRF Creations

Avery, you are the most amazing girl.
Remember that you can do anything you set your mind to.
Remain bold, remain strong, and remain YOU.

Mom and Dad love you to the moon and back.

TABLE OF CONTENTS

NOTE FROM THE AUTHOR	1
AFFIRMATIONS	5
HOW TO USE THIS JOURNAL	6
Goal Setting	6
Accomplishments I am proud of	7
How I Helped My Teammates	7
Favorite Gymnastics Moments	8
Hydration	8
Monthly Reflection	9
Why I Am Grateful	9
What I Loved About Gymnastics This Month	9
Thank You	9
GOAL SETTING TIPS	10
VISION BOARD	10
GOALS FOR THE YEAR	12
QUARTERLY BENCHMARK GOALS	13
BEGIN YOUR WEEKLY JOURNALING	14
MEET MEMORIES	161
ACKNOWLEDGMENTS	172
ABOUT THE AUTHOR	173
SUBSCRIBE	174
OTHER WORKS BY THE AUTHOR	175

NOTE FROM THE AUTHOR

Congratulations! You fell in love with gymnastics. Guess what? That's awesome! Gymnastics can be rewarding and exciting. As you practice and prepare for meets, or special events remember to go back to the things that you enjoy most.

Throughout your gymnastics journey, you will have many ups and downs. Embrace them. There will be days when you don't enjoy practice, or your coaches are pushing you harder than you like. These feelings are part of the journey. They are part of growth. Just like your body experiences growing pains that hurt, so do your thinking and emotions. Journaling your steps along the way can help remind you of the roadblocks, accomplishments, and successful moments.

You will sometimes struggle to land your full turn on the beam or complete your front tuck successfully. Once again, these hurdles are part of the journey. There will be times when you don't make the level you want or don't accomplish a skill as fast as your teammates. These setbacks are all part of your journey. Gymnastics is WHAT you do; gymnastics does not define WHO you are!

Who you are is how you treat yourself and others. Be kind to yourself. Have faith and confidence in the journey. Do the work to achieve your goals, and eventually, you will succeed. Be someone upon whom your teammates and gymnastics friends rely. They are going through the same journey and share a lot of your fears.

Be coachable! This concept is important. Your coaches aren't criticizing you because they don't like you. They do like you and want to help you grow. Listen to them and be grateful for the constructive feedback that will make you a better gymnast. If you are lucky enough to have an excellent coach, she or he will also help you be a better person.

Know that you are going to make mistakes along the way. Mistakes are 100% OKAY! Mistakes are how you learn, so forgive yourself. Capitalize on your mistakes to do better in the future. Forgive others for their mistakes.

Remember that not everyone will be kind. Attitude is part of life and part of learning. Over time, you will know that you cannot control how others act and react, but you can control your actions and reactions. Treat others as you want to be treated and work every day to be the best gymnast and person you can be.

I hope this gymnastics journal will help you to cherish the memories. I hope you will reflect after your season and see that you accomplished many goals, grew as a person and a gymnast, and believe how exceptional you are!

Always be YOU-niquely YOU!

Much love,

Stacy

You can do anything you put your mind to.

Do the work!
Have faith!
Believe in yourself!
Obstacles are temporary!

I believe in YOU,
go do great things!

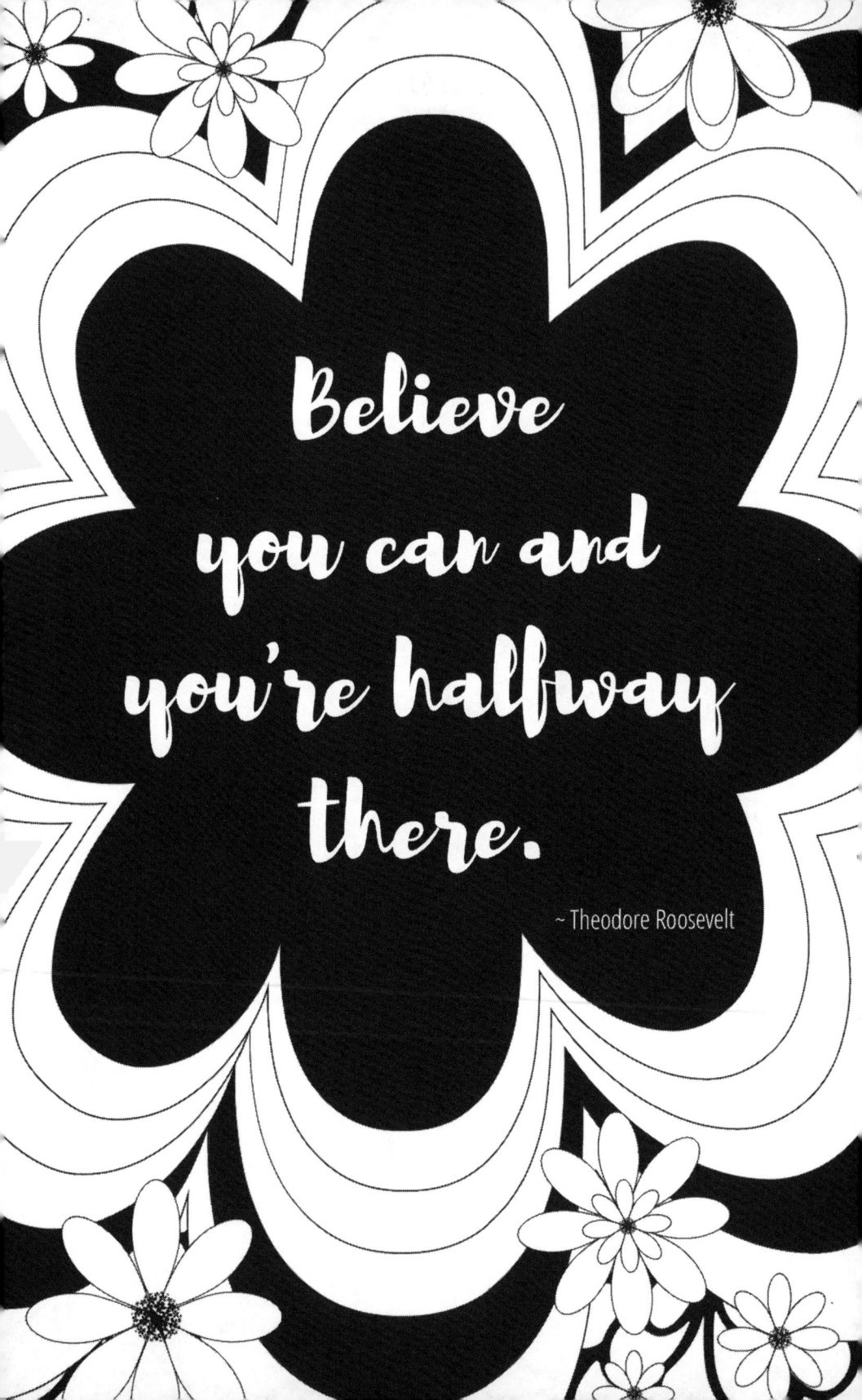

AFFIRMATIONS

I am strong.
I am resilient.
I am capable.
I am worthy.
I am beautiful.
I am kind.
I am smart.
I am proud of what I have accomplished.
I am hardworking.
I am dedicated.
My potential is limitless.
I feel good about myself.
I feel good about my body.
I have a purpose.
Who I am makes a difference.
I am in charge of my success.
I can accomplish anything.
I take pride in my work.
I am courageous.
I am confident.
I love myself.
I set goals, and I reach them.
I am a good teammate.
I am a good gymnast.
I am proud to be me.
I am enough.
I am unique.
I am valuable.
I take pride in my progress.
I make the most of each moment.

HOW TO USE THIS JOURNAL
RECORD YOUR PROGRESS

GOAL SETTING

Setting goals for yourself is essential to your success if you want to continue growing and learning. Goals are milestones or achievements along the way. The cool thing about goals is understanding that even if you don't reach every goal, you grew while pursuing your goals, and that growth, my fellow gymnast, is what matters most.

At the beginning of this journal, you will set significant goals that you want to accomplish by the end of your gymnastics season. You will then set quarterly benchmark goals. You can achieve your benchmark goals in short periods of time. Benchmark goals keep you on track to achieve your year-end goal. Each month you will set monthly goals that are baby steps along your journey.

Let's recap for clarity one more time!

- What are my significant goals for the season?
- How can I set myself up for success in order to reach those goals?
- What are my quarterly benchmark goals?
- What monthly goals can I set to push me in the right direction along my journey?
-

Set your monthly goals at the beginning of each month with your quarterly goals in mind. For example, let's say one of your yearly goals is to complete a technically sound giant on the bars. Set a quarterly goal to consistently complete a free hip handstand and to strengthen your arm and chest muscles

Your monthly goals may be to attend an extra practice each week, complete conditioning exercises four times each week and remind yourself daily that you can achieve your goal. These are the goals you choose. Again, break down your significant goals into bite-size goals.

Now, let's set some goals!

ACCOMPLISHMENTS I AM PROUD OF

Each week jot down your small wins for the week. It is essential to document small victories along the way. They remind you of the work you put in each week. These accomplishments may be physical skills you gained or mental growth, like keeping a positive attitude all week. Perhaps getting enough rest or drinking plenty of water each day improved. Whatever makes YOU proud and feel good, write it down; you will appreciate it when you look back later. No accomplishment is too small.

HOW I HELPED MY TEAMMATES

You rise by lifting others. The fantastic benefit of being part of a team or group is that you have other people working to achieve the same goals. You may have team goals to consider in your journey, so think about those goals when planning. What are you doing to help your team succeed? Also, consider how you are contributing to your teammates' individual successes. We all need someone to cheer us on and root for us if we feel down or don't want to do the extra work. How are you contributing to your team culture? Are you a negative apple that sours the bunch, or are you a light that shines as an example to those around you? What kind of teammate do you want to be?

In this journal section, you can jot down both the good and the bad. News flash: no one is perfect—not even you. You are meant only to be perfectly unique. Maybe one week you're the negative apple, and the next week you're the shining light. THAT'S OKAY! Don't be afraid to spread compliments to those around you. Tell them if they are doing well, crushing their vault, or nailing a new skill.

Acknowledge your teammates' success! Write about it! Determine how YOU can contribute to helping those around you rise. Sometimes you need help from others to help you grow, which is OKAY too!

FAVORITE GYMNASTICS MOMENTS

Just as the title suggests, what activities did you enjoy in class or practice during the week? Examples could be learning a skill on the beam or making a new friend. You might have enjoyed a recent activity or team bonding game you played. Perhaps you had a guest coach, and you enjoyed working with him. It is easy to get lost in competition results, but the true gifts of gymnastics are far beyond the apparatus. Make notations each week of your fun memories and moments.

HYDRATION

Each day, you can choose to hold yourself accountable by marking down how many glasses of water you've had for the day. Your body needs water, period. Water hydrates your skin, and it can help with your digestion. Water helps boost your energy and provides fuel to your muscles. As a gymnast, you need the proper fuel for your body to function correctly.

You are consistently working out and pushing your body to reach new heights each day. Treat yourself right and drink plenty of water. Fruits and veggies are good too, but we will save that topic for another day.

MONTHLY REFLECTION

The reflection page is an opportunity for you to look back on the month. Where did you succeed? Where could you do better? Who impacted your month? Who did you impact? This page offers a moment to think back, write notes, and grow.

WHY I AM GRATEFUL

Have an attitude of gratitude. Research shows that gratitude is associated with greater happiness. Use this page to jot down what you are most grateful for throughout the month in your life, gymnastics, or school. Express your gratitude to others.

THINGS I LOVE ABOUT GYMNASTICS

Exactly as the title suggests, use this page to draw pictures or make notes about what you love about gymnsatics each month.

THANK YOU

Write notes to people who impacted you during the last month. You can keep the notes private or send them. Either way, it is good to write down your thanks and remember who helped you along your journey.

GOAL SETTING TIPS

Set SMART goals
- Specific - Make sure your goals are well defined.
- ·Measurable - Consider how you will measure the achievement of your goals. For example, if your goal is to have better leaps. How will you determine if your leaps have improved?
- ·Achievable - You want to set goals that are realistic.
- ·Relevant – Set goals that apply to your team and the level you compete You can set some "fun" goals, but understand how these goals won't impact your team.
- Time focused - Set a deadline to achieve your goals.

Lucky for you, your My Gymnastics Journal helps you to set SMART goals!

VISION BOARD

A vision board is anything that inspires you. You can draw, doodle, and cut and paste pictures or quotes. Choose things that you want to be, feel, or do. Allow your mind to see yourself inside your vision board. For example, perhaps you want to be a collegiate gymnast. Fill up your vision board with images or words that represent your chosen school. Maybe your goal is to be a coach someday, then fill your board with moments when your coaches made you feel amazing. Perhaps you want to attend the Olympics, then you'll want to fill your vision board with drawings of Olympic symbols and pictures of your favorite Olympians. I think you get the point now. There is no wrong way to do a vision board. It's yours, so have fun!

VISION BOARD

GOALS FOR THE YEAR

QUARTERLY BENCHMARK GOALS

PERSONAL GOALS

TEAM GOALS

ACADEMIC GOALS

WEEK:_____ DATE:_____/_____/_____

GOALS FOR THE MONTH

◎ PERSONAL GOALS

TEAM GOALS

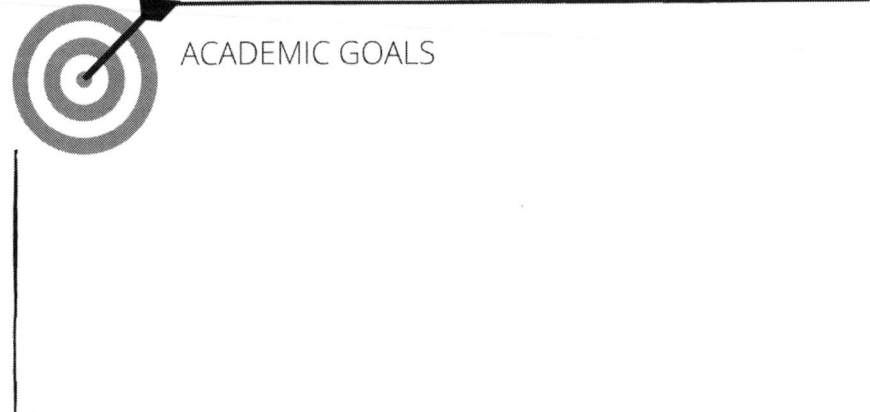

ACADEMIC GOALS

WEEK:_____ DATE:_____/_____/_____

HYDRATION

Week 1

Week 2

Week 3

Week 4

WEEK:_____ DATE:_____/_____/_____

Below is an example of how to fill out the weekly pages.

ACCOMPLISHMENTS I'M PROUD OF
I finally did a giant on the strap bar. I am so excited to do it again next practice

HOW I HELPED MY TEAMMATES
Lisa was struggling to do her leg lifts, so I stayed and did them with her, even though I already did mine.

FAVORITE GYMNASTICS MOMENTS
Swinging around the strap bar doing my giant felt awesome. I've cried several times thinking I would never get it. It feels good to have worked through that.

PRACTICE NOTES
Don't forget to get my grips and tiger paws out of my locker for the meet this weekend.
Give mom the meet info.
I'm so excited for Ozone invitational.
Mentally go through my routines and remember to tuck my toe under after my turn!

WEEK:_____ DATE:_____/_____/_____

Start each day with a grateful heart, and you will be fulfilled.

ACCOMPLISHMENTS I'M PROUD OF

HOW I HELPED MY TEAMMATES

FAVORITE GYMNASTICS MOMENTS

PRACTICE NOTES

WEEK:_____   DATE:_____/_____/_____

Failures are learning opportunities along the way to success.

ACCOMPLISHMENTS I'M PROUD OF
_____
_____
_____

HOW I HELPED MY TEAMMATES
_____
_____
_____

FAVORITE GYMNASTICS MOMENTS
_____
_____
_____

PRACTICE NOTES
_____

_____
_____
_____
_____
_____

WEEK:_____   DATE:_____/_____/_____

Cherish the time with teammates and friends.

ACCOMPLISHMENTS I'M PROUD OF

HOW I HELPED MY TEAMMATES

FAVORITE GYMNASTICS MOMENTS

PRACTICE NOTES

WEEK:_____   DATE:_____/_____/_____

Make sure to eat your fruits and veggies.

ACCOMPLISHMENTS I'M PROUD OF
_____
_____
_____

HOW I HELPED MY TEAMMATES
_____
_____
_____

FAVORITE GYMNASTICS MOMENTS
_____
_____
_____

PRACTICE NOTES
_____
_____
_____
_____
_____
_____

20

WEEK:_____   DATE:_____/_____/_____

CELEBRATE MONTHLY PRACTICE WINS

Practice wins don't always have to be about gaining new skills. Wins could be that you welcomed newcomers to your team and made them feel comfortable at a new gym. Wins could be that you stayed positive even though you were having a hard day. Celebrating EVERY win is crucial to success and growth!

HOW DID MY SKILLS & STRENGTH GROW?
_____
_____
_____

HOW DID MY CHARACTER GROW?
_____
_____
_____
_____

HOW DID I GROW MENTALLY?
_____
_____
_____

AFFIRMATIONS IN ACTION - visualize my goals as I say the statements below out loud.

When I did my _____, I felt _____
When my team _____, I felt _____

WEEK:_____   DATE:_____/_____/_____

MONTHLY REFLECTION

Self-Reflection is looking back so that looking forward can be even clearer.

DID I REACH MY GOALS? If yes, what steps did I take to reach my goals? If not, what could I have done differently?

_____
_____
_____
_____

I WAS MOST POSITIVELY IMPACTED BY...

_____
_____
_____
_____

I POSITIVELY IMPACTED...

_____
_____
_____

IN THE COMING WEEKS, I AM LOOKING FORWARD TO...

_____
_____
_____
_____

WEEK:_____   DATE:_____/_____/_____

I AM GRATEFUL

WEEK:_____ DATE:_____/_____/_____

WHAT I LOVED ABOUT GYMNASTICS THIS MONTH

WEEK:_____   DATE:_____/_____/_____

THANK YOU

thank you

WEEK:_____   DATE:_____/_____/_____

GOALS FOR THE MONTH

PERSONAL GOALS

TEAM GOALS

ACADEMIC GOALS

Creativity is intelligence having fun!
Design your perfect leo!

WEEK:_____ DATE:_____/_____/_____

HYDRATION

Week 1

Week 2

Week 3

Week 4

WEEK:_____ DATE:_____/_____/_____

Dance for fun today in your room blasting your favorite song.

ACCOMPLISHMENTS I'M PROUD OF
_____
_____
_____

HOW I HELPED MY TEAMMATES
_____
_____
_____

FAVORITE GYMNASTICS MOMENTS
_____
_____
_____

PRACTICE NOTES
_____
_____
_____
_____
_____
_____
_____

WEEK:_____   DATE:_____/_____/_____

Who you are makes a difference.

ACCOMPLISHMENTS I'M PROUD OF
_____
_____
_____

HOW I HELPED MY TEAMMATES
_____
_____
_____
_____

FAVORITE GYMNASTICS MOMENTS
_____
_____
_____
_____

PRACTICE NOTES
_____
_____
_____
_____
_____
_____

WEEK:_____ DATE:_____/_____/_____

You matter!

ACCOMPLISHMENTS I'M PROUD OF
_____
_____
_____

HOW I HELPED MY TEAMMATES
_____
_____
_____

FAVORITE GYMNASTICS MOMENTS
_____
_____
_____

PRACTICE NOTES
_____
_____
_____
_____
_____
_____
_____

WEEK:_____ DATE:_____/_____/_____

It's good to count to ten before you react.

ACCOMPLISHMENTS I'M PROUD OF
_____
_____
_____

HOW I HELPED MY TEAMMATES
_____
_____
_____

FAVORITE GYMNASTICS MOMENTS
_____
_____
_____

PRACTICE NOTES
_____
_____
_____
_____
_____

WEEK:_____   DATE:_____/_____/_____

CELEBRATE MONTHLY PRACTICE WINS

Practice wins don't always have to be about gaining new skills. Wins could be that you welcomed newcomers to your team and made them feel comfortable at a new gym. Wins could be that you stayed positive even though you were having a hard day. Celebrating EVERY win is crucial to success and growth!

HOW DID MY SKILLS & STRENGTH GROW?
_____
_____
_____

HOW DID MY CHARACTER GROW?
_____
_____
_____

HOW DID I GROW MENTALLY?
_____
_____
_____

AFFIRMATIONS IN ACTION - visualize my goals as I say the statements below out loud.

When I did my _____, I felt _____
When my team _____, I felt _____

WEEK:_____   DATE:_____/_____/_____

MONTHLY REFLECTION

By knowing yourself you gain persepctive and wisdom.

DID I REACH MY GOALS? If yes, what steps did I take to reach my goals? If not, what could I have done differently?

_____
_____
_____
_____

I WAS MOST POSITIVELY IMPACTED BY...

_____
_____
_____
_____

I POSITIVELY IMPACTED...

_____
_____
_____
_____

IN THE COMING WEEKS, I AM LOOKING FORWARD TO...

_____
_____
_____
_____

WEEK:_____   DATE:_____/_____/_____

I AM GRATEFUL

WEEK:_____   DATE:_____/_____/_____

WHAT I LOVED ABOUT GYMNASTICS THIS MONTH

WEEK:_____   DATE:_____/_____/_____

THANK YOU

thank you

WEEK:_____   DATE:_____/_____/_____

GOALS FOR THE MONTH

PERSONAL GOALS

TEAM GOALS

ACADEMIC GOALS

WEEK:_____ DATE:_____/_____/_____

HYDRATION

Week 1

Week 2

Week 3

Week 4

WEEK:_____ DATE:_____/_____/_____

It's okay to get frustrated. Take a deep breath.

ACCOMPLISHMENTS I'M PROUD OF
_____
_____
_____

HOW I HELPED MY TEAMMATES
_____
_____
_____

FAVORITE GYMNASTICS MOMENTS
_____
_____
_____

PRACTICE NOTES
_____
_____
_____
_____
_____
_____

WEEK:_____ DATE:_____/_____/_____

Do something nice for someone else today.

ACCOMPLISHMENTS I'M PROUD OF

HOW I HELPED MY TEAMMATES

FAVORITE GYMNASTICS MOMENTS

PRACTICE NOTES

WEEK:_____ DATE:_____/_____/_____

Watch some gymnastics videos; you'll learn from them.

ACCOMPLISHMENTS I'M PROUD OF

HOW I HELPED MY TEAMMATES

FAVORITE GYMNASTICS MOMENTS

PRACTICE NOTES

WEEK:_____   DATE:_____/_____/_____

Make sure you're drinking plenty of water.

ACCOMPLISHMENTS I'M PROUD OF

HOW I HELPED MY TEAMMATES

FAVORITE GYMNASTICS MOMENTS

PRACTICE NOTES

WEEK:_____   DATE:_____/_____/_____

Be sure to properly warm up and stretch your muscles.

ACCOMPLISHMENTS I'M PROUD OF
_____
_____
_____

HOW I HELPED MY TEAMMATES
_____
_____
_____
_____

FAVORITE GYMNASTICS MOMENTS
_____
_____
_____
_____

PRACTICE NOTES
_____
_____
_____
_____
_____
_____
_____

WEEK:_____ DATE:_____/_____/_____

CELEBRATE MONTHLY PRACTICE WINS

Practice wins don't always have to be about gaining new skills. Wins could be that you welcomed newcomers to your team and made them feel comfortable at a new gym. Wins could be that you stayed positive even though you were having a hard day. Celebrating EVERY win is crucial to success and growth!

HOW DID MY SKILLS & STRENGTH GROW?

_____

_____

_____

HOW DID MY CHARACTER GROW?

_____

_____

_____

HOW DID I GROW MENTALLY?

_____

_____

_____

AFFIRMATIONS IN ACTION - visualize my goals as I say the statements below out loud.

When I did my _____, I felt _____
When my team _____, I felt _____

WEEK:_____   DATE:_____/_____/_____

MONTHLY REFLECTION

How we speak to others is a reflection of ourselves.

DID I REACH MY GOALS? If yes, what steps did I take to reach my goals? If not, what could I have done differently?

_____
_____
_____
_____

I WAS MOST POSITIVELY IMPACTED BY...

_____
_____
_____
_____

I POSITIVELY IMPACTED...

_____
_____
_____
_____

IN THE COMING WEEKS, I AM LOOKING FORWARD TO...

_____
_____
_____
_____

WEEK:_____   DATE:_____/_____/_____

I AM GRATEFUL

WEEK:_____ DATE:_____/_____/_____

WHAT I LOVED ABOUT GYMNASTICS THIS MONTH

WEEK:_____   DATE:_____/_____/_____

THANK YOU

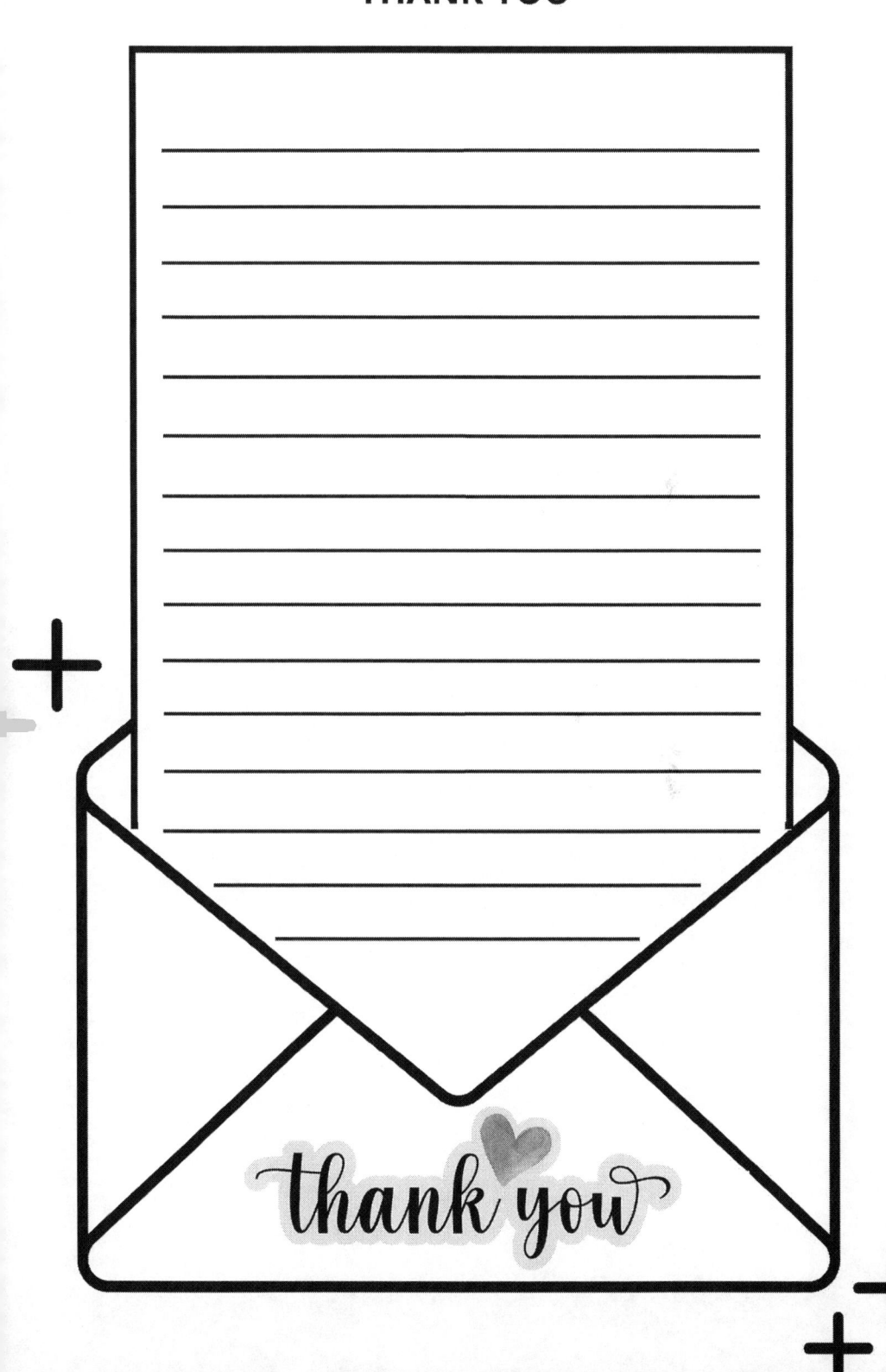

QUARTERLY BENCHMARK GOALS

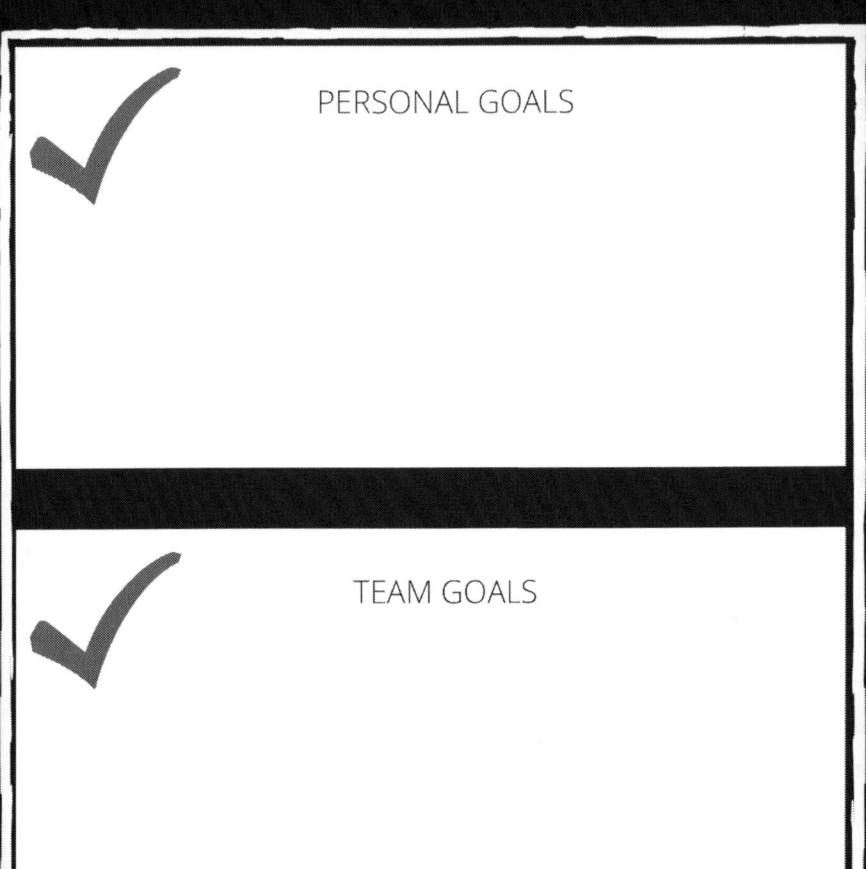

✓ PERSONAL GOALS

✓ TEAM GOALS

✓ ACADEMIC GOALS

The best preparation for tomorrow is doing your best today.

WEEK:_____   DATE:_____/_____/_____

GOALS FOR THE MONTH

PERSONAL GOALS

TEAM GOALS

ACADEMIC GOALS

WEEK:_____ DATE:_____/_____/_____

HYDRATION

Week 1

Week 2

Week 3

Week 4

WEEK:_____   DATE:_____/_____/_____

Today is a new day, let go of past moments that bothered you.

ACCOMPLISHMENTS I'M PROUD OF
_____
_____
_____

HOW I HELPED MY TEAMMATES
_____
_____
_____

FAVORITE GYMNASTICS MOMENTS
_____
_____
_____

PRACTICE NOTES
_____
_____
_____
_____
_____
_____
_____

WEEK:_____ DATE:_____/_____/_____

Find a good book and read a chapter a day.

ACCOMPLISHMENTS I'M PROUD OF

HOW I HELPED MY TEAMMATES

FAVORITE GYMNASTICS MOMENTS

PRACTICE NOTES

WEEK:_____ DATE:_____/_____/_____

LIVE - LOVE - GYMNASTICS

ACCOMPLISHMENTS I'M PROUD OF
_____
_____
_____

HOW I HELPED MY TEAMMATES
_____
_____
_____

FAVORITE GYMNASTICS MOMENTS
_____
_____
_____

PRACTICE NOTES
_____
_____
_____
_____
_____
_____

WEEK:_____   DATE:_____/_____/_____

Doing your homework should be a priority.

ACCOMPLISHMENTS I'M PROUD OF
_____
_____
_____

HOW I HELPED MY TEAMMATES
_____
_____
_____

FAVORITE GYMNASTICS MOMENTS
_____
_____
_____

PRACTICE NOTES
_____
_____
_____
_____
_____

WEEK:_____   DATE:_____/_____/_____

CELEBRATE MONTHLY PRACTICE WINS

Practice wins don't always have to be about gaining new skills. Wins could be that you welcomed newcomers to your team and made them feel comfortable at a new gym. Wins could be that you stayed positive even though you were having a hard day. Celebrating EVERY win is crucial to success and growth!

HOW DID MY SKILLS & STRENGTH GROW?
_____
_____
_____

HOW DID MY CHARACTER GROW?
_____
_____
_____

HOW DID I GROW MENTALLY?
_____
_____
_____

AFFIRMATIONS IN ACTION - visualize my goals as I say the statements below out loud.

When I did my _____, I felt _____
When my team _____, I felt _____

WEEK:_____   DATE:_____/_____/_____

MONTHLY REFLECTION

Gain insight into yourself through reflective thinking.

DID I REACH MY GOALS? If yes, what steps did I take to reach my goals? If not, what could I have done differently?

_____
_____
_____
_____

I WAS MOST POSITIVELY IMPACTED BY...

_____
_____
_____
_____

I POSITIVELY IMPACTED...

_____
_____
_____
_____

IN THE COMING WEEKS, I AM LOOKING FORWARD TO...

_____
_____
_____
_____

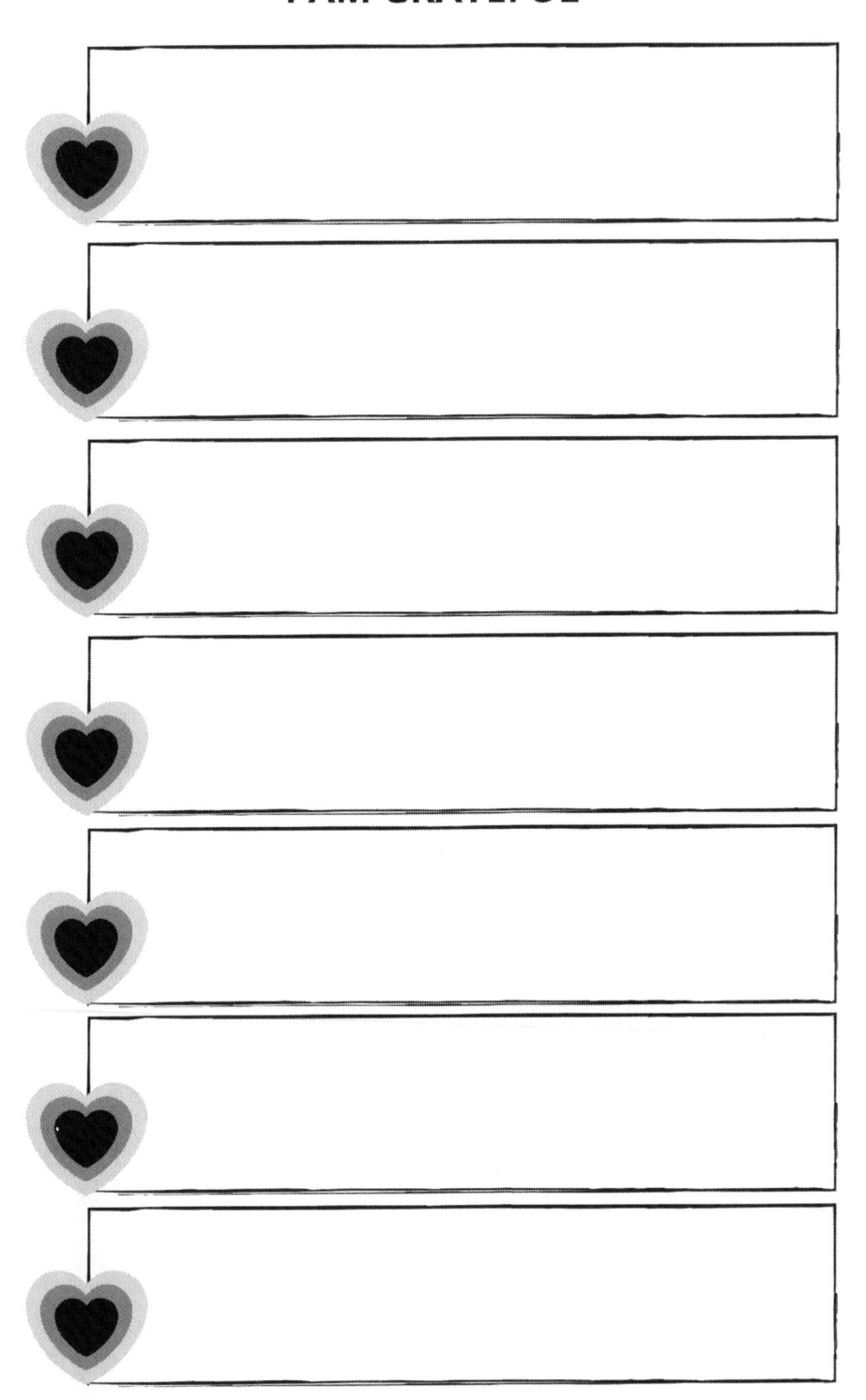

WEEK:_____ DATE:_____/_____/_____

I AM GRATEFUL

WEEK:_____ DATE:_____/_____/_____

WHAT I LOVED ABOUT GYMNASTICS THIS MONTH

WEEK:_____   DATE:_____/_____/_____

THANK YOU

WEEK:_____   DATE:_____/_____/_____

GOALS FOR THE MONTH

PERSONAL GOALS

TEAM GOALS

ACADEMIC GOALS

WEEK:_____   DATE:_____/_____/_____

HYDRATION

Week 1

Week 2

Week 3

Week 4

WEEK:_____ DATE:_____/_____/_____

Practice like you've never won. Compete like you've never lost.

ACCOMPLISHMENTS I'M PROUD OF
_____
_____
_____

HOW I HELPED MY TEAMMATES
_____
_____
_____

FAVORITE GYMNASTICS MOMENTS
_____
_____
_____

PRACTICE NOTES
_____
_____
_____
_____
_____
_____
_____

WEEK:_____ DATE:_____/_____/_____

Your worth is not in the opinions of others.

ACCOMPLISHMENTS I'M PROUD OF

HOW I HELPED MY TEAMMATES

FAVORITE GYMNASTICS MOMENTS

PRACTICE NOTES

WEEK:_____   DATE:_____/_____/_____

The world deserves who were created to be.

ACCOMPLISHMENTS I'M PROUD OF
_____
_____
_____

HOW I HELPED MY TEAMMATES
_____
_____
_____

FAVORITE GYMNASTICS MOMENTS
_____
_____
_____

PRACTICE NOTES
_____
_____
_____
_____
_____
_____
_____

WEEK:_____ DATE:_____/_____/_____

Your character is who you are on the inside.

ACCOMPLISHMENTS I'M PROUD OF
_____
_____
_____

HOW I HELPED MY TEAMMATES
_____
_____
_____

FAVORITE GYMNASTICS MOMENTS
_____
_____
_____

PRACTICE NOTES
_____
_____
_____
_____
_____
_____

WEEK:_____   DATE:_____/_____/_____

CELEBRATE MONTHLY PRACTICE WINS

Practice wins don't always have to be about gaining new skills. Wins could be that you welcomed newcomers to your team and made them feel comfortable at a new gym. Wins could be that you stayed positive even though you were having a hard day. Celebrating EVERY win is crucial to success and growth!

HOW DID MY SKILLS & STRENGTH GROW?
_____
_____
_____
_____

HOW DID MY CHARACTER GROW?
_____
_____
_____
_____

HOW DID I GROW MENTALLY?
_____
_____
_____
_____

AFFIRMATIONS IN ACTION - visualize my goals as I say the statements below out loud.

When I did my _____, I felt _____
When my team _____, I felt _____

WEEK:_____   DATE:_____/_____/_____

MONTHLY REFLECTION

Remember that you cannot fail at being yourself.

DID I REACH MY GOALS? If yes, what steps did I take to reach my goals? If not, what could I have done differently?

_____
_____
_____
_____

I WAS MOST POSITIVELY IMPACTED BY...

_____
_____
_____
_____

I POSITIVELY IMPACTED...

_____
_____
_____
_____

IN THE COMING WEEKS, I AM LOOKING FORWARD TO...

_____
_____
_____
_____

WEEK:_____   DATE:_____/_____/_____

I AM GRATEFUL

WEEK:_____ DATE:_____/_____/_____

WHAT I LOVED ABOUT GYMNASTICS THIS MONTH

WEEK:_____   DATE:_____/_____/_____

THANK YOU

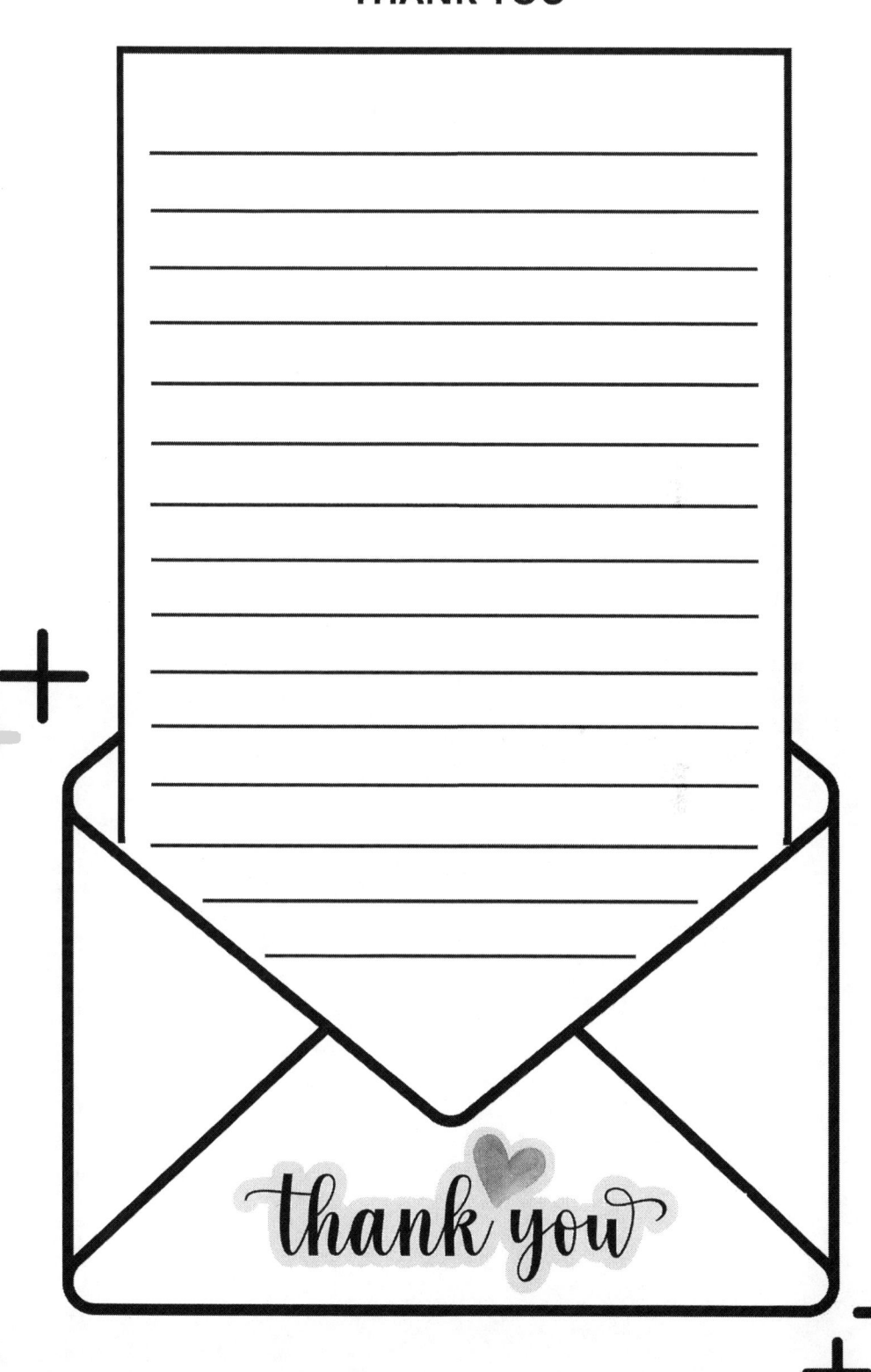

WEEK:_____   DATE:_____/_____/_____

GOALS FOR THE MONTH

PERSONAL GOALS

TEAM GOALS

ACADEMIC GOALS

WEEK:_____ DATE:_____/_____/_____

HYDRATION

Week 1

Week 2

Week 3

Week 4

WEEK:_____   DATE:_____/_____/_____

You can achieve anything you put your mind to.

ACCOMPLISHMENTS I'M PROUD OF
_____
_____
_____

HOW I HELPED MY TEAMMATES
_____
_____
_____
_____

FAVORITE GYMNASTICS MOMENTS
_____
_____
_____
_____

PRACTICE NOTES
_____
_____
_____
_____
_____
_____
_____

WEEK:_____   DATE:_____/_____/_____

When you get knocked down, get back up, and keep going.

ACCOMPLISHMENTS I'M PROUD OF

HOW I HELPED MY TEAMMATES

FAVORITE GYMNASTICS MOMENTS

PRACTICE NOTES

WEEK:_____   DATE:_____/_____/_____

> Dig deep, find out who you are and really get to know her.

ACCOMPLISHMENTS I'M PROUD OF
_____
_____
_____

HOW I HELPED MY TEAMMATES
_____
_____
_____

FAVORITE GYMNASTICS MOMENTS
_____
_____
_____

PRACTICE NOTES
_____
_____
_____
_____
_____
_____

WEEK:_____ DATE:_____/_____/_____

Love yourself.

ACCOMPLISHMENTS I'M PROUD OF
_____
_____
_____

HOW I HELPED MY TEAMMATES
_____
_____
_____

FAVORITE GYMNASTICS MOMENTS
_____
_____
_____

PRACTICE NOTES
_____
_____
_____
_____
_____
_____

WEEK:_____ DATE:_____ / _____ / _____

Nothing easy is worth achieving. Do the work.

ACCOMPLISHMENTS I'M PROUD OF

HOW I HELPED MY TEAMMATES

FAVORITE GYMNASTICS MOMENTS

PRACTICE NOTES

WEEK:_____   DATE:_____/_____/_____

CELEBRATE MONTHLY PRACTICE WINS

Practice wins don't always have to be about gaining new skills. Wins could be that you welcomed newcomers to your team and made them feel comfortable at a new gym. Wins could be that you stayed positive even though you were having a hard day. Celebrating EVERY win is crucial to success and growth!

HOW DID MY SKILLS & STRENGTH GROW?
_____
_____
_____
_____

HOW DID MY CHARACTER GROW?
_____
_____
_____
_____

HOW DID I GROW MENTALLY?
_____
_____
_____
_____

AFFIRMATIONS IN ACTION - visualize my goals as I say the statements below out loud.

When I did my _____, I felt _____
When my team _____, I felt _____

WEEK:_____ DATE:_____/_____/_____

MONTHLY REFLECTION

Everyone has faults. Know your faults and own them.

DID I REACH MY GOALS? If yes, what steps did I take to reach my goals? If not, what could I have done differently?

_____
_____
_____
_____

I WAS MOST POSITIVELY IMPACTED BY...

_____
_____
_____
_____

I POSITIVELY IMPACTED...

_____
_____
_____
_____

IN THE COMING WEEKS, I AM LOOKING FORWARD TO...

_____
_____
_____
_____

WEEK:_____   DATE:_____/_____/_____

I AM GRATEFUL

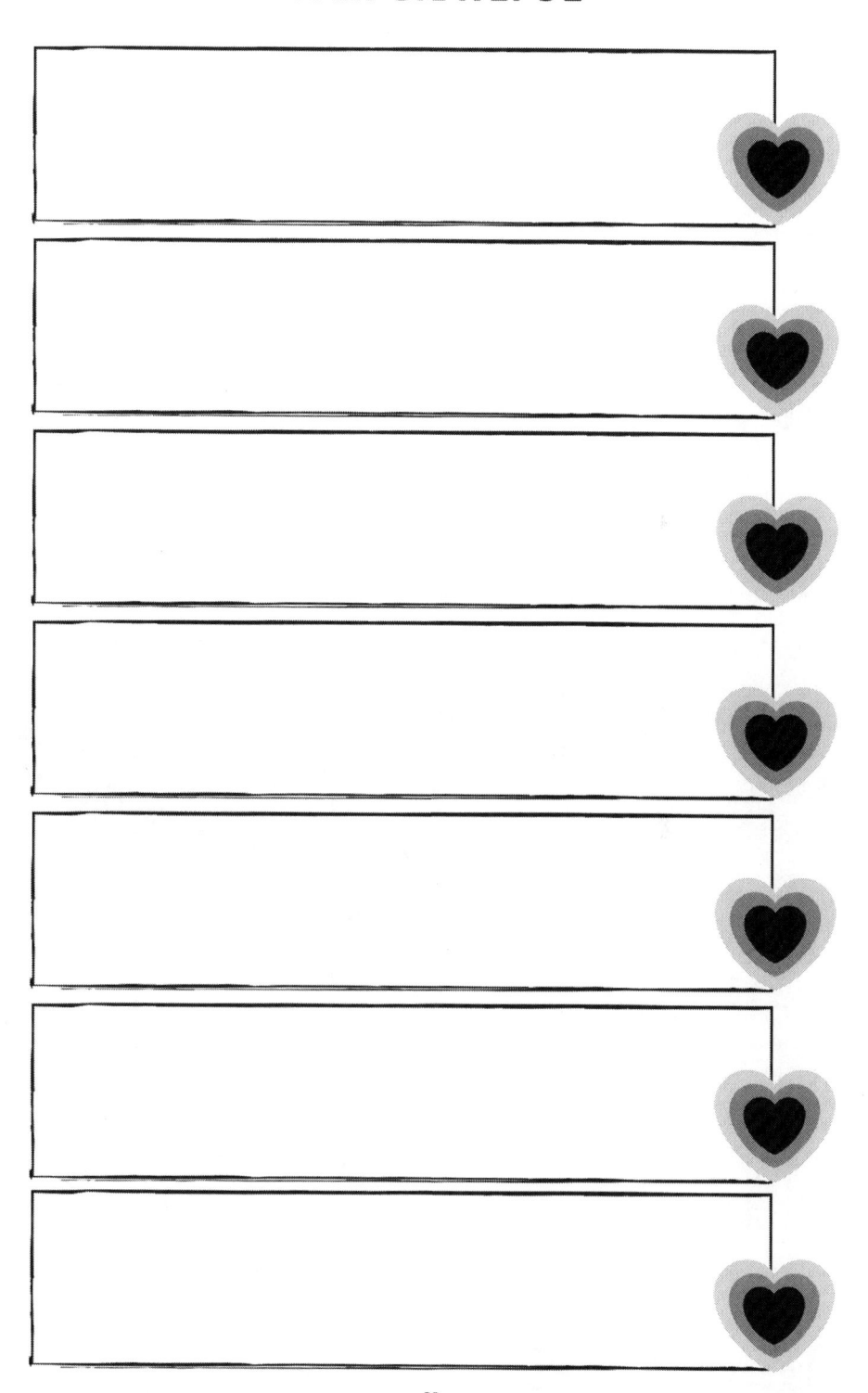

WEEK:_____   DATE:_____/_____/_____

WHAT I LOVED ABOUT GYMNASTICS THIS MONTH

WEEK:_____   DATE:_____/_____/_____

THANK YOU

thank you

QUARTERLY BENCHMARK GOALS

✓ PERSONAL GOALS

✓ TEAM GOALS

✓ ACADEMIC GOALS

Plant the seeds of your dreams,

and watch them grow!

WEEK:_____ DATE:_____/_____/_____

GOALS FOR THE MONTH

PERSONAL GOALS

TEAM GOALS

ACADEMIC GOALS

WEEK:_____ DATE:_____/_____/_____

HYDRATION

Week 1

Week 2

Week 3

Week 4

WEEK:_____   DATE:_____/_____/_____

Be humble. Arrogance is unbecoming.

ACCOMPLISHMENTS I'M PROUD OF
_____
_____
_____

HOW I HELPED MY TEAMMATES
_____
_____
_____

FAVORITE GYMNASTICS MOMENTS
_____
_____
_____

PRACTICE NOTES
_____
_____
_____
_____
_____
_____

WEEK:_____   DATE:_____/_____/_____

Be genuine in your thoughts, actions, and feelings.

ACCOMPLISHMENTS I'M PROUD OF

HOW I HELPED MY TEAMMATES

FAVORITE GYMNASTICS MOMENTS

PRACTICE NOTES

WEEK:_____   DATE:_____/_____/_____

You rise by lifting others.

ACCOMPLISHMENTS I'M PROUD OF
_____
_____
_____

HOW I HELPED MY TEAMMATES
_____
_____
_____

FAVORITE GYMNASTICS MOMENTS
_____
_____
_____

PRACTICE NOTES
_____
_____
_____
_____
_____
_____
_____
_____

WEEK:_____ DATE:_____/_____/_____

You can't buy happiness. You must find it within.

ACCOMPLISHMENTS I'M PROUD OF
_____
_____
_____

HOW I HELPED MY TEAMMATES
_____
_____
_____

FAVORITE GYMNASTICS MOMENTS
_____
_____
_____

PRACTICE NOTES
_____
_____
_____
_____
_____
_____

WEEK:_____ DATE:_____/_____/_____

CELEBRATE MONTHLY PRACTICE WINS

Practice wins don't always have to be about gaining new skills. Wins could be that you welcomed newcomers to your team and made them feel comfortable at a new gym. Wins could be that you stayed positive even though you were having a hard day. Celebrating EVERY win is crucial to success and growth!

HOW DID MY SKILLS & STRENGTH GROW?

_____
_____
_____
_____

HOW DID MY CHARACTER GROW?

_____
_____
_____
_____

HOW DID I GROW MENTALLY?

_____
_____
_____
_____

AFFIRMATIONS IN ACTION - visualize my goals as I say the statements below out loud.

When I did my _____, I felt _____
When my team _____, I felt _____

WEEK:_____ DATE:_____/_____/_____

MONTHLY REFLECTION

Reflecting on the past can be the key to the future.

DID I REACH MY GOALS? If yes, what steps did I take to reach my goals? If not, what could I have done differently?

_____
_____
_____
_____

I WAS MOST POSITIVELY IMPACTED BY...

_____
_____
_____
_____

I POSITIVELY IMPACTED...

_____
_____
_____
_____

IN THE COMING WEEKS, I AM LOOKING FORWARD TO...

_____
_____
_____

WEEK:_____   DATE:_____/_____/_____

I AM GRATEFUL

WEEK:_____   DATE:_____/_____/_____

WHAT I LOVED ABOUT GYMNASTICS THIS MONTH

WEEK:_____   DATE:_____/_____/_____

THANK YOU

She believed she could FLY SO SHE DID

WEEK:_____ DATE:_____/_____/_____

GOALS FOR THE MONTH

PERSONAL GOALS

TEAM GOALS

ACADEMIC GOALS

WEEK:_____   DATE:_____/_____/_____

HYDRATION

Week 1

Week 2

Week 3

Week 4

WEEK:_____   DATE:_____/_____/_____

If at first, you don't succeed. Keep working, success is near.

ACCOMPLISHMENTS I'M PROUD OF
_____
_____
_____

HOW I HELPED MY TEAMMATES
_____
_____
_____
_____

FAVORITE GYMNASTICS MOMENTS
_____
_____
_____
_____

PRACTICE NOTES
_____
_____
_____
_____
_____
_____

WEEK:_____   DATE:_____/_____/_____

Things don't always go your way. Keep going anyway.

ACCOMPLISHMENTS I'M PROUD OF
_____
_____
_____

HOW I HELPED MY TEAMMATES
_____
_____
_____

FAVORITE GYMNASTICS MOMENTS
_____
_____
_____

PRACTICE NOTES
_____
_____
_____
_____
_____
_____

WEEK:_____   DATE:_____/_____/_____

People aren't always kind. Be kind anyway.

ACCOMPLISHMENTS I'M PROUD OF
_____
_____
_____

HOW I HELPED MY TEAMMATES
_____
_____
_____

FAVORITE GYMNASTICS MOMENTS
_____
_____
_____

PRACTICE NOTES
_____
_____
_____
_____
_____
_____
_____

WEEK:_____ DATE:_____/_____/_____

Every day is what you make, so make it great.

ACCOMPLISHMENTS I'M PROUD OF
_____
_____
_____

HOW I HELPED MY TEAMMATES
_____
_____
_____

FAVORITE GYMNASTICS MOMENTS
_____
_____
_____

PRACTICE NOTES
_____
_____
_____
_____
_____

WEEK:_____   DATE:_____/_____/_____

CELEBRATE MONTHLY PRACTICE WINS

Practice wins don't always have to be about gaining new skills. Wins could be that you welcomed newcomers to your team and made them feel comfortable at a new gym. Wins could be that you stayed positive even though you were having a hard day. Celebrating EVERY win is crucial to success and growth!

HOW DID MY SKILLS & STRENGTH GROW?

_____
_____
_____

HOW DID MY CHARACTER GROW?

_____
_____
_____

HOW DID I GROW MENTALLY?

_____
_____
_____

AFFIRMATIONS IN ACTION - visualize my goals as I say the statements below out loud.

When I did my _____, I felt _____
When my team _____, I felt_____

WEEK:_____   DATE:_____/_____/_____

MONTHLY REFLECTION

Self reflection brings awareness.

DID I REACH MY GOALS? If yes, what steps did I take to reach my goals? If not, what could I have done differently?

_____
_____
_____
_____

I WAS MOST POSITIVELY IMPACTED BY...

_____
_____
_____
_____

I POSITIVELY IMPACTED...

_____
_____
_____
_____

IN THE COMING WEEKS, I AM LOOKING FORWARD TO...

_____
_____
_____
_____

WEEK:_____   DATE:_____/_____/_____

I AM GRATEFUL

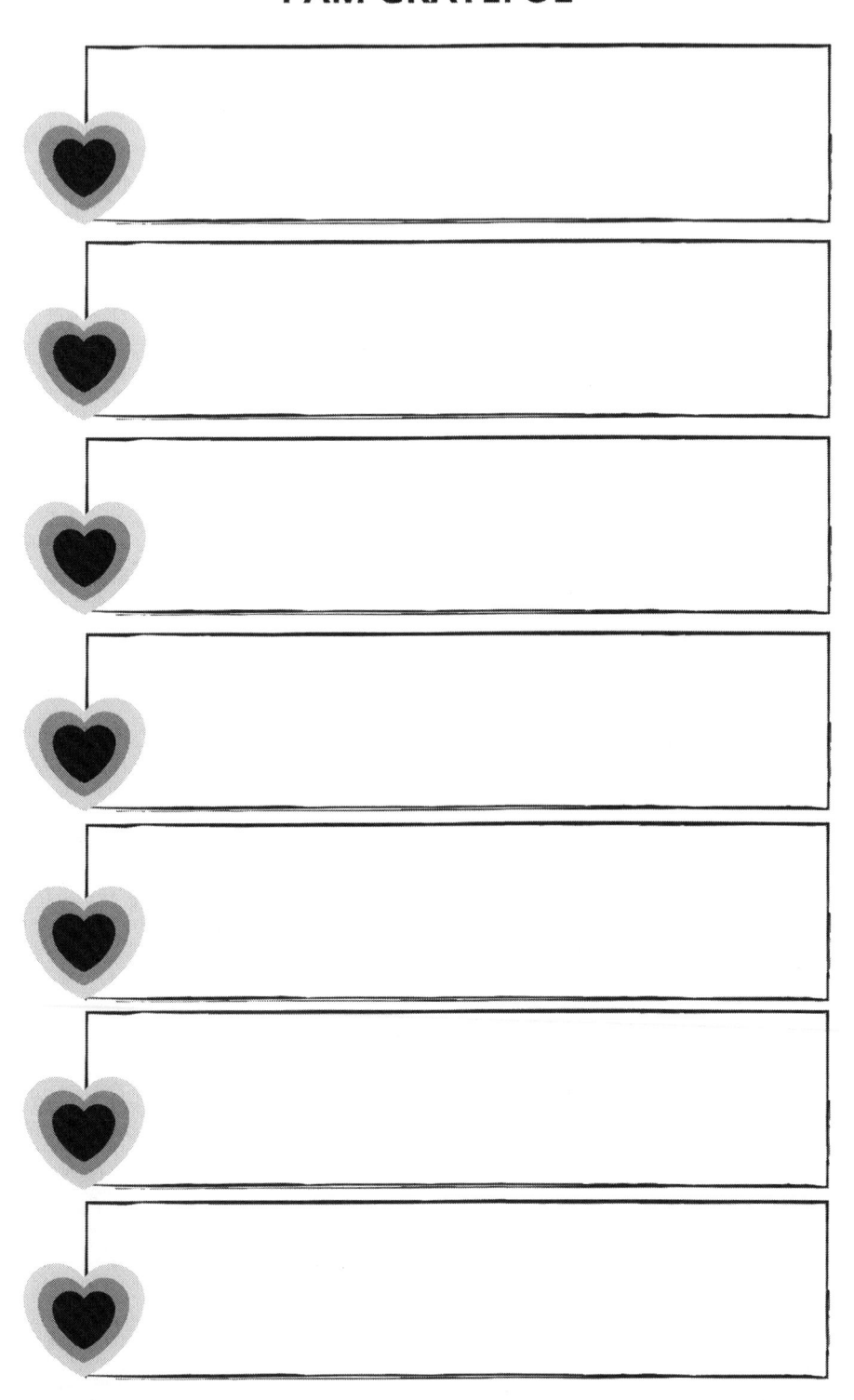

WEEK:_____   DATE:_____/_____/_____

WHAT I LOVED ABOUT GYMNASTICS THIS MONTH

WEEK:_____   DATE:_____/_____/_____

THANK YOU

WEEK:_____   DATE:_____/_____/_____

GOALS FOR THE MONTH

PERSONAL GOALS

TEAM GOALS

ACADEMIC GOALS

WEEK:_____   DATE:_____/_____/_____

HYDRATION

Week 1

Week 2

Week 3

Week 4

WEEK:_____ DATE:_____/_____/_____

Record your meets and review with honest eyes.

ACCOMPLISHMENTS I'M PROUD OF
_____
_____
_____

HOW I HELPED MY TEAMMATES
_____
_____
_____

FAVORITE GYMNASTICS MOMENTS
_____
_____
_____

PRACTICE NOTES
_____
_____
_____
_____
_____
_____

WEEK:_____   DATE:_____/_____/_____

A bad day is a fleeting moment in time, tomorrow is a new day.

ACCOMPLISHMENTS I'M PROUD OF
_____
_____
_____

HOW I HELPED MY TEAMMATES
_____
_____
_____

FAVORITE GYMNASTICS MOMENTS
_____
_____
_____

PRACTICE NOTES
_____
_____
_____
_____
_____

WEEK:_____ DATE:_____/_____/_____

Believe and you will achieve.

ACCOMPLISHMENTS I'M PROUD OF
_____
_____
_____

HOW I HELPED MY TEAMMATES
_____
_____
_____
_____

FAVORITE GYMNASTICS MOMENTS
_____
_____
_____
_____

PRACTICE NOTES
_____
_____
_____
_____
_____
_____
_____

WEEK:_____   DATE:_____/_____/_____

Remember what you love most about gymnastics.

ACCOMPLISHMENTS I'M PROUD OF
_____
_____
_____

HOW I HELPED MY TEAMMATES
_____
_____
_____

FAVORITE GYMNASTICS MOMENTS
_____
_____
_____

PRACTICE NOTES
_____
_____
_____
_____
_____

WEEK:_____   DATE:_____/_____/_____

Your success is completely up to you.

ACCOMPLISHMENTS I'M PROUD OF
_____
_____

HOW I HELPED MY TEAMMATES
_____
_____
_____

FAVORITE GYMNASTICS MOMENTS
_____
_____
_____

PRACTICE NOTES
_____
_____
_____
_____
_____
_____

WEEK:_____   DATE:_____/_____/_____

CELEBRATE MONTHLY PRACTICE WINS

Practice wins don't always have to be about gaining new skills. Wins could be that you welcomed newcomers to your team and made them feel comfortable at a new gym. Wins could be that you stayed positive even though you were having a hard day. Celebrating EVERY win is crucial to success and growth!

HOW DID MY SKILLS & STRENGTH GROW?

_____
_____
_____
_____

HOW DID MY CHARACTER GROW?

_____
_____
_____
_____

HOW DID I GROW MENTALLY?

_____
_____
_____
_____

AFFIRMATIONS IN ACTION - visualize my goals as I say the statements below out loud.

When I did my _____, I felt _____
When my team _____, I felt _____

WEEK:_____   DATE:_____/_____/_____

MONTHLY REFLECTION

The more you reflect the more you learn about yourself.

DID I REACH MY GOALS? If yes, what steps did I take to reach my goals? If not, what could I have done differently?

_____
_____
_____
_____

I WAS MOST POSITIVELY IMPACTED BY...

_____
_____
_____
_____

I POSITIVELY IMPACTED...

_____
_____
_____
_____

IN THE COMING WEEKS, I AM LOOKING FORWARD TO...

_____
_____
_____
_____

WEEK:_____   DATE:_____/_____/_____

I AM GRATEFUL

WEEK:_____ DATE:_____/_____/_____

WHAT I LOVED ABOUT GYMNASTICS THIS MONTH

WEEK:_____   DATE:_____/_____/_____

THANK YOU

Happiness never decreases by being shared.

~ Gautama

QUARTERLY BENCHMARK GOALS

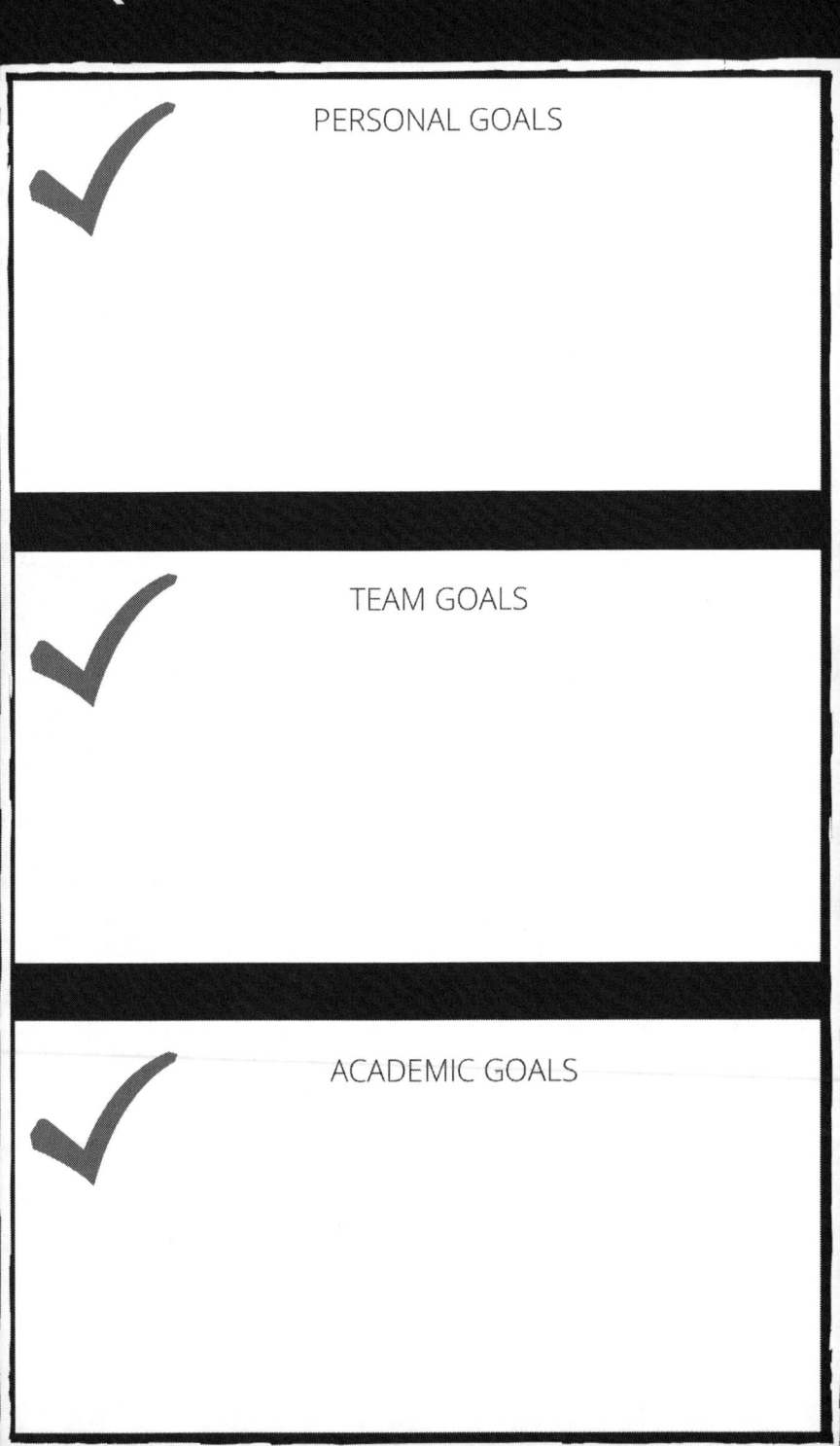

✓ PERSONAL GOALS

✓ TEAM GOALS

✓ ACADEMIC GOALS

WEEK:_____   DATE:_____/_____/_____

GOALS FOR THE MONTH

PERSONAL GOALS

TEAM GOALS

ACADEMIC GOALS

WEEK:_____   DATE:_____/_____/_____

HYDRATION

Week 1

Week 2

Week 3

Week 4

WEEK:_____ DATE:_____/_____/_____

Your results at a meet do not define your progress.

ACCOMPLISHMENTS I'M PROUD OF
_____
_____
_____

HOW I HELPED MY TEAMMATES
_____
_____
_____
_____

FAVORITE GYMNASTICS MOMENTS
_____
_____
_____
_____

PRACTICE NOTES
_____
_____
_____
_____
_____
_____
_____
_____

WEEK: _____   DATE: _____ / _____ / _____

Celebrate your accomplishments.

ACCOMPLISHMENTS I'M PROUD OF
_____
_____
_____

HOW I HELPED MY TEAMMATES
_____
_____
_____

FAVORITE GYMNASTICS MOMENTS
_____
_____
_____

PRACTICE NOTES
_____
_____
_____
_____
_____
_____

WEEK:_____   DATE:_____/_____/_____

Shine bright like the star that you are.

ACCOMPLISHMENTS I'M PROUD OF
_____
_____
_____

HOW I HELPED MY TEAMMATES
_____
_____
_____

FAVORITE GYMNASTICS MOMENTS
_____
_____
_____

PRACTICE NOTES
_____
_____
_____
_____
_____
_____

WEEK:_____   DATE:_____/_____/_____

Have faith in yourself and you will succeed.

ACCOMPLISHMENTS I'M PROUD OF
_____
_____
_____

HOW I HELPED MY TEAMMATES
_____
_____
_____

FAVORITE GYMNASTICS MOMENTS
_____
_____
_____

PRACTICE NOTES
_____
_____
_____
_____
_____

WEEK:_____   DATE:_____/_____/_____

CELEBRATE MONTHLY PRACTICE WINS

Practice wins don't always have to be about gaining new skills. Wins could be that you welcomed newcomers to your team and made them feel comfortable at a new gym. Wins could be that you stayed positive even though you were having a hard day. Celebrating EVERY win is crucial to success and growth!

HOW DID MY SKILLS & STRENGTH GROW?
_____
_____
_____

HOW DID MY CHARACTER GROW?
_____
_____
_____

HOW DID I GROW MENTALLY?
_____
_____
_____

AFFIRMATIONS IN ACTION - visualize my goals as I say the statements below out loud.

When I did my _____, I felt _____
When my team _____, I felt _____

WEEK:_____   DATE:_____/_____/_____

MONTHLY REFLECTION

Sometimes life is two steps foward and one step back.

DID I REACH MY GOALS? If yes, what steps did I take to reach my goals? If not, what could I have done differently?

_____
_____
_____
_____

I WAS MOST POSITIVELY IMPACTED BY...

_____
_____
_____
_____

I POSITIVELY IMPACTED...

_____
_____
_____
_____

IN THE COMING WEEKS, I AM LOOKING FORWARD TO...

_____
_____
_____
_____

WEEK:_____   DATE:_____/_____/_____

I AM GRATEFUL

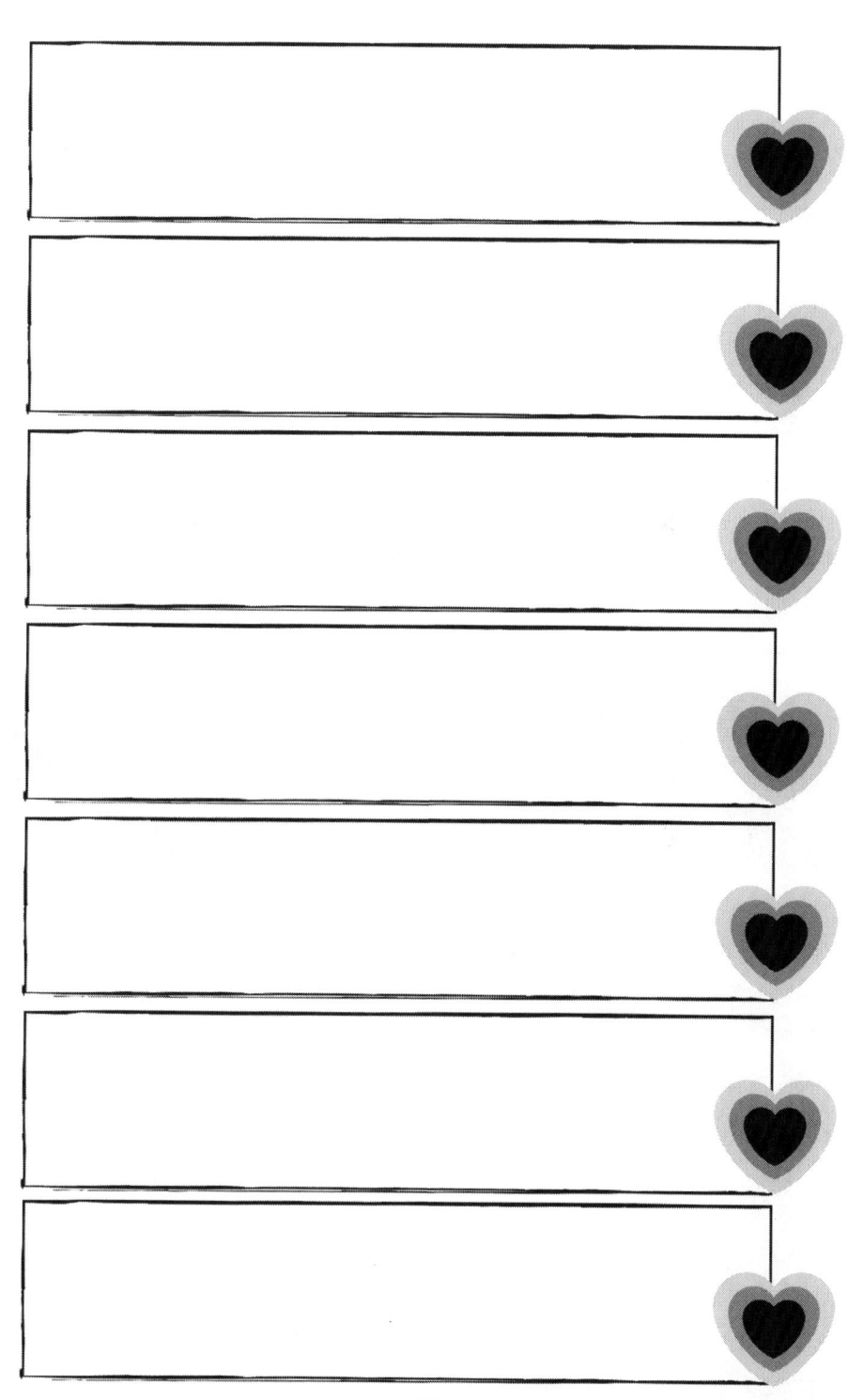

WEEK:_____   DATE:_____/_____/_____

WHAT I LOVED ABOUT GYMNASTICS THIS MONTH

WEEK:_____   DATE:_____/_____/_____

THANK YOU

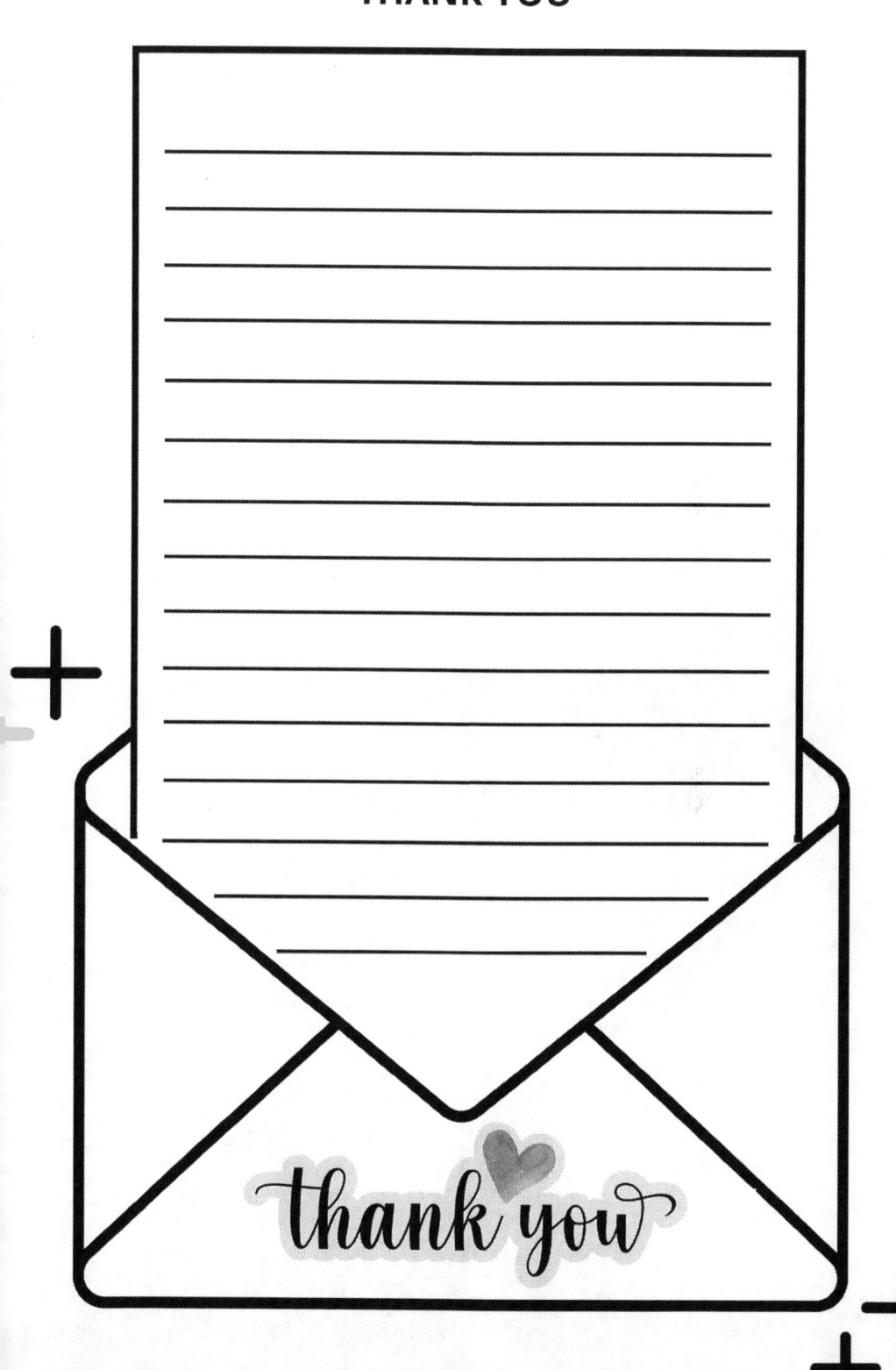

You don't know how far you can go until you go there!

~ Stacy Rowe

powered by zone

WEEK:_____   DATE:_____/_____/_____

GOALS FOR THE MONTH

PERSONAL GOALS

TEAM GOALS

ACADEMIC GOALS

WEEK:_____ DATE:_____/_____/_____

HYDRATION

Week 1

Week 2

Week 3

Week 4

WEEK:_____   DATE:_____/_____/_____

Don't just do the work when others are watching.

ACCOMPLISHMENTS I'M PROUD OF

_____
_____
_____

HOW I HELPED MY TEAMMATES

_____
_____
_____
_____

FAVORITE GYMNASTICS MOMENTS

_____
_____
_____
_____

PRACTICE NOTES

_____
_____
_____
_____
_____
_____
_____

WEEK:_____   DATE:_____/_____/_____

Stay focused on your goals.

ACCOMPLISHMENTS I'M PROUD OF
_____
_____
_____

HOW I HELPED MY TEAMMATES
_____
_____
_____

FAVORITE GYMNASTICS MOMENTS
_____
_____
_____

PRACTICE NOTES
_____
_____
_____
_____
_____
_____

WEEK:_____   DATE:_____/_____/_____

Don't be afraid to dream big.

ACCOMPLISHMENTS I'M PROUD OF
_____
_____
_____

HOW I HELPED MY TEAMMATES
_____
_____
_____

FAVORITE GYMNASTICS MOMENTS
_____
_____
_____

PRACTICE NOTES
_____
_____
_____
_____
_____
_____

WEEK: _____   DATE: _____ / _____ / _____

Teammates can be the best friends. Enjoy the moment.

ACCOMPLISHMENTS I'M PROUD OF
_____
_____
_____

HOW I HELPED MY TEAMMATES
_____
_____
_____

FAVORITE GYMNASTICS MOMENTS
_____
_____
_____

PRACTICE NOTES
_____
_____
_____
_____
_____
_____

WEEK:_____   DATE:_____/_____/_____

CELEBRATE MONTHLY PRACTICE WINS

Practice wins don't always have to be about gaining new skills. Wins could be that you welcomed newcomers to your team and made them feel comfortable at a new gym. Wins could be that you stayed positive even though you were having a hard day. Celebrating EVERY win is crucial to success and growth!

HOW DID MY SKILLS & STRENGTH GROW?
_____
_____
_____

HOW DID MY CHARACTER GROW?
_____
_____
_____

HOW DID I GROW MENTALLY?
_____
_____
_____

AFFIRMATIONS IN ACTION - visualize my goals as I say the statements below out loud.

When I did my _____, I felt _____
When my team _____, I felt _____

WEEK:_____   DATE:_____/_____/_____

MONTHLY REFLECTION

The greatest fault is not being conscious of your own faults.

DID I REACH MY GOALS? If yes, what steps did I take to reach my goals? If not, what could I have done differently?

_____
_____
_____
_____

I WAS MOST POSITIVELY IMPACTED BY...

_____
_____
_____
_____

I POSITIVELY IMPACTED...

_____
_____
_____
_____

IN THE COMING WEEKS, I AM LOOKING FORWARD TO...

_____
_____
_____
_____

WEEK:_____   DATE:_____/_____/_____

I AM GRATEFUL

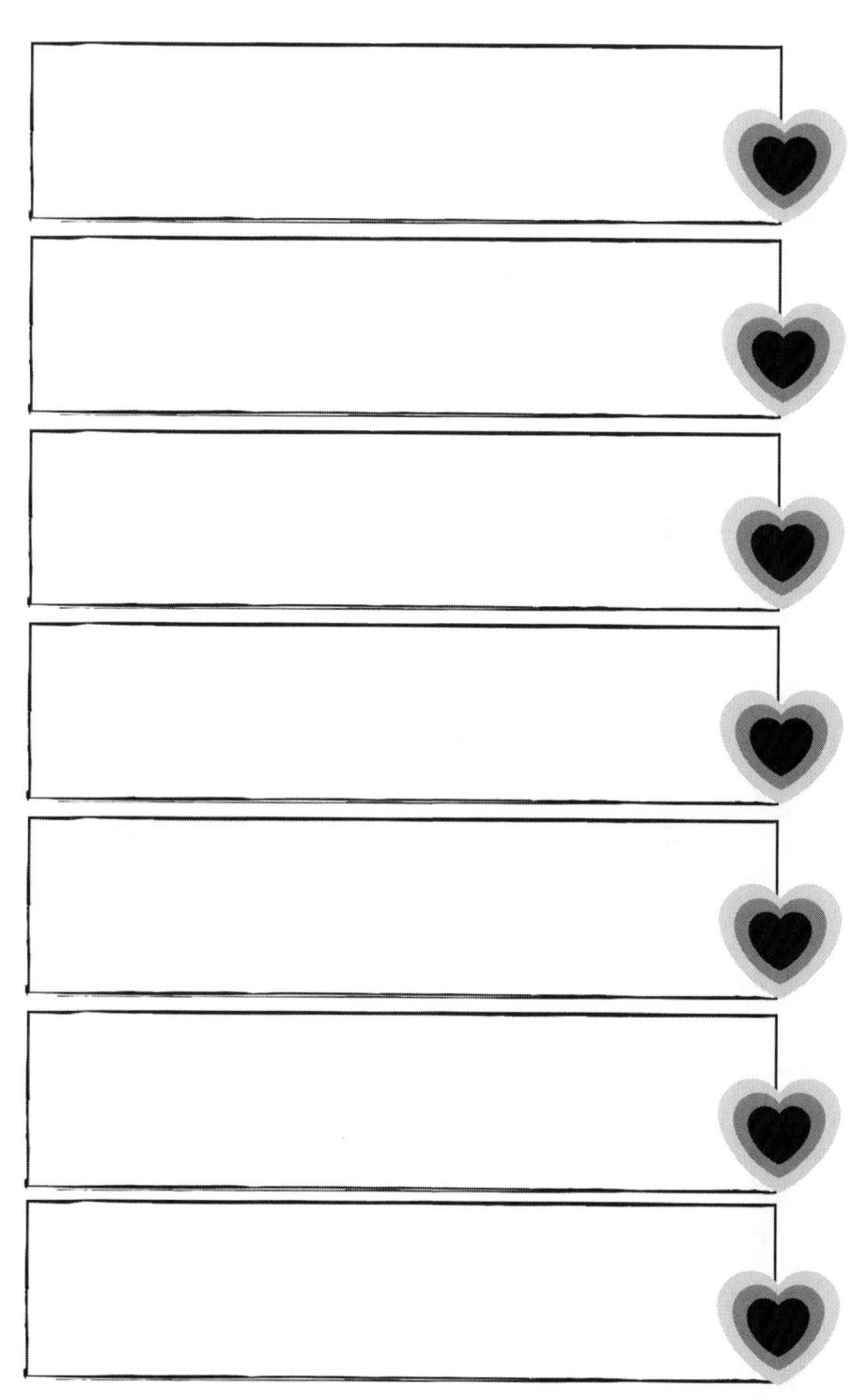

WEEK:_____ DATE:_____/_____/_____

WHAT I LOVED ABOUT GYMNASTICS THIS MONTH

WEEK:_____ DATE:_____/_____/_____

THANK YOU

thank you

WEEK:_____   DATE:_____/_____/_____

GOALS FOR THE MONTH

PERSONAL GOALS

TEAM GOALS

ACADEMIC GOALS

WEEK:_____ DATE:_____/_____/_____

HYDRATION

Week 1

Week 2

Week 3

Week 4

WEEK:_____   DATE:_____/_____/_____

The lessons along the way are the real prize.

ACCOMPLISHMENTS I'M PROUD OF
_____
_____
_____

HOW I HELPED MY TEAMMATES
_____
_____
_____

FAVORITE GYMNASTICS MOMENTS
_____
_____
_____

PRACTICE NOTES
_____
_____
_____
_____
_____
_____

WEEK:_____   DATE:_____/_____/_____

There is never a time to stop learning.

ACCOMPLISHMENTS I'M PROUD OF
_____
_____
_____

HOW I HELPED MY TEAMMATES
_____
_____
_____

FAVORITE GYMNASTICS MOMENTS
_____
_____
_____

PRACTICE NOTES
_____
_____
_____
_____
_____

WEEK:_____   DATE:_____ /_____ /_____

Put in the work and the results will come.

ACCOMPLISHMENTS I'M PROUD OF
_____
_____
_____

HOW I HELPED MY TEAMMATES
_____
_____
_____

FAVORITE GYMNASTICS MOMENTS
_____
_____
_____

PRACTICE NOTES
_____
_____
_____
_____
_____
_____
_____

WEEK:_____   DATE:_____/_____/_____

You're on your OWN journey, don't compare yourself to others.

ACCOMPLISHMENTS I'M PROUD OF
_____
_____
_____

HOW I HELPED MY TEAMMATES
_____
_____
_____
_____

FAVORITE GYMNASTICS MOMENTS
_____
_____
_____
_____

PRACTICE NOTES
_____
_____
_____
_____
_____
_____

WEEK:_____   DATE:_____/_____/_____

Reflect on your year and enjoy the growth.

ACCOMPLISHMENTS I'M PROUD OF
_____
_____
_____

HOW I HELPED MY TEAMMATES
_____
_____
_____

FAVORITE GYMNASTICS MOMENTS
_____
_____
_____

PRACTICE NOTES
_____
_____
_____
_____
_____
_____
_____

WEEK:_____   DATE:_____/_____/_____

CELEBRATE MONTHLY PRACTICE WINS

Practice wins don't always have to be about gaining new skills. Wins could be that you welcomed newcomers to your team and made them feel comfortable at a new gym. Wins could be that you stayed positive even though you were having a hard day. Celebrating EVERY win is crucial to success and growth!

HOW DID MY SKILLS & STRENGTH GROW?

_____
_____
_____

HOW DID MY CHARACTER GROW?

_____
_____
_____

HOW DID I GROW MENTALLY?

_____
_____
_____

AFFIRMATIONS IN ACTION - visualize my goals as I say the statements below out loud.

When I did my _____, I felt _____
When my team _____, I felt _____

WEEK:_____   DATE:_____/_____/_____

MONTHLY REFLECTION

Learn from the past to gain perspective on the future.

DID I REACH MY GOALS? If yes, what steps did I take to reach my goals? If not, what could I have done differently?

_____
_____
_____
_____

I WAS MOST POSITIVELY IMPACTED BY...

_____
_____
_____
_____

I POSITIVELY IMPACTED...

_____
_____
_____
_____

IN THE COMING WEEKS, I AM LOOKING FORWARD TO...

_____
_____
_____
_____

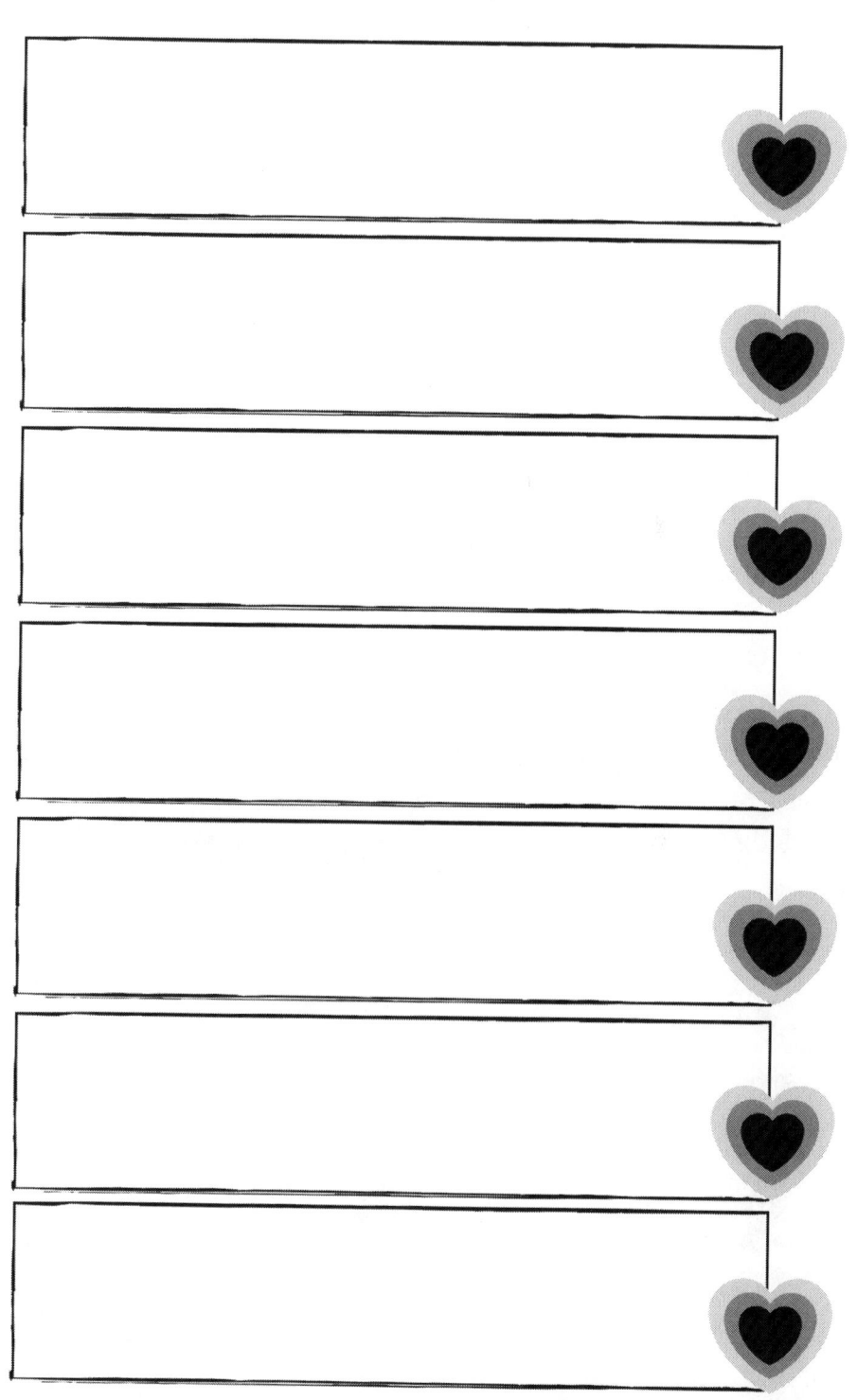

WEEK:_____   DATE:_____/_____/_____

I AM GRATEFUL

WEEK:_____   DATE:_____/_____/_____

WHAT I LOVED ABOUT GYMNASTICS THIS MONTH

WEEK:_____   DATE:_____/_____/_____

THANK YOU

You only get out of gymnastics what you give to gymnastics.

MEET MEMORIES

EVENT NAME: _____

CITY: _____ DATE: _____

SCORES

TEAM PLACEMENT

MEET REFLECTIONS

ALL AROUND

NEW FRIENDS

FUN TIMES

MEET MEMORIES

EVENT NAME: _____

CITY: _____ DATE: _____

SCORES

TEAM PLACEMENT

MEET REFLECTIONS

ALL AROUND
_____

NEW FRIENDS

FUN TIMES

MEET MEMORIES

EVENT NAME: _____

CITY: _____ DATE: _____

SCORES

- _____
- _____
- _____
- _____

ALL AROUND
_____

TEAM PLACEMENT

_____

MEET REFLECTIONS

_____
_____
_____
_____
_____
_____
_____

NEW FRIENDS

_____
_____
_____
_____
_____
_____
_____
_____
_____

FUN TIMES

_____
_____
_____
_____
_____
_____
_____
_____
_____

MEET MEMORIES

EVENT NAME: _____
CITY: _____ DATE: _____

SCORES

TEAM PLACEMENT

MEET REFLECTIONS

ALL AROUND

NEW FRIENDS

FUN TIMES

MEET MEMORIES

EVENT NAME: _____

CITY: _____ DATE: _____

SCORES

_____

_____

_____

_____

ALL AROUND

_____

TEAM PLACEMENT

_____

MEET REFLECTIONS

_____
_____
_____
_____
_____
_____
_____

NEW FRIENDS

_____
_____
_____
_____
_____
_____
_____
_____

FUN TIMES

_____
_____
_____
_____
_____
_____
_____
_____

Wherever you go, go with your heart.

MEET MEMORIES

EVENT NAME: _____
CITY: _____ DATE: _____

SCORES

TEAM PLACEMENT

MEET REFLECTIONS

ALL AROUND

NEW FRIENDS

FUN TIMES

MEET MEMORIES

EVENT NAME: _____

CITY: _____ DATE: _____

SCORES

TEAM PLACEMENT

MEET REFLECTIONS

ALL AROUND

NEW FRIENDS

FUN TIMES

MEET MEMORIES

EVENT NAME: _____

CITY: _____ DATE: _____

SCORES

TEAM PLACEMENT

MEET REFLECTIONS

ALL AROUND

NEW FRIENDS

FUN TIMES

MEET MEMORIES

EVENT NAME: _____

CITY: _____ DATE: _____

SCORES

TEAM PLACEMENT

MEET REFLECTIONS

ALL AROUND

NEW FRIENDS

FUN TIMES

Every CHAMPION was once a beginner that didn't quit.

ACKNOWLEDGMENTS

To all the gymnastics coaches and gym owners, thank you for sharing your passion for gymnastics. Thank you for making the sacrifices necessary to provide safe and wonderful learning environments for all kids who want to do gymnastics. I know the grind, and I appreciate all that you do.

To my former teachers, coaches, and instructors thank you for everything you taught me through the years. I wouldn't be who I am today without your guidance and mentorship.

To my husband, thank you. Thank you for being supportive of my crazy ideas and ventures, for late-night chats, and for always encouraging me.

To my children, I love you more than any words can express. Everything I do is for you.

To my former athletes, thank you for inspiring me every day to be a better mentor, teacher, and coach. I am so proud of each and every one of you.

To my friends, brothers, sisters, nieces, and nephews, thank you for being the best. I am so lucky to say you are my friends and my family. Your love and support mean the world to me.

To Ozone Leotards, thank you for allowing me to use the Ozone brand.

ABOUT THE AUTHOR

S.R. Fabrico

I was born and raised a Yankee who loves New York style pizza and Philly cheesesteaks. I was introduced to the amazing world of Southern barbecue after moving to Tennessee, where I live with my husband and two children. My family is my main priority. Everything I do is for them. I attended college in the 1990s and earned a degree in mathematics with a minor in secondary education.

I went on to own a cheer gym and dance studio, where I coached cheerleading and dance for over twenty years and won a Hip Hop Dance World Championship. I was named USASF Dance Coach of the year in 2014 and currently host dance events throughout the U.S. with Stage 8 Dance Brands.

Helping athletes grow as young adults has always been my passion. I am honored to provide a journal for gymnasts that may positively assist them along their journeys.

I published my award winning debut novel (a women's coming of age fiction) The Secrets We Conceal in March of 2022, and I am currently working on a second novel. I took a joyful break from fiction writing to create the MY JOURNAL SERIES.

Let's get social @srfabrico_author Interested in bulk order discounts email srfabricoauthor@gmail.com

Stay up to date on recent news and information and subscribe to my newsletter at www.srfabrico.com

Subscribe to S.R. Fabrico's newsletter

My Gymnastics Journal is available for teams at bulk order discounts!

Email srfabricoauthor@gmail.com

OTHER WORKS BY S.R. FABRICO

My Cheer Journal

My Dance Journal

My Swim Journal

COMING SOON

My Soccer Journal

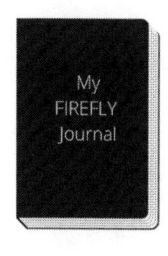

The Firefly Journal
A journal for woman

Would you like a My Journal in a sport that isn't available?
Email srfabricoauthor@gmail.com

Made in the USA
Columbia, SC
01 February 2025